Fact, Value, and Perception

Fact, Value, and Perception is a collection of eleven essays by former colleagues and students of Charles A. Baylis, who was for many years Professor and Chairman of the Department of Philosophy, Duke University. Professor Baylis wrote an important book, *Ethics: Principles of Wise Choice*, as well as many articles, and his wide-ranging influence in the fields of ethics, philosophy of perception, and theory of knowledge and logic is demonstrated in several of the essays contained in this volume.

Fact, Value, and Perception

Essays in Honor of
Charles A. Baylis

Paul Welsh, *Editor*

Duke University Press
Durham, N.C.
1 9 7 5

L.C.C. card number 74–75987

I.S.B.N. 0–8223–0321–3

PRINTED IN THE UNITED STATES OF
AMERICA BY KINGSPORT PRESS

1887818

Contents

Preface

Charles Augustus Baylis was born in Portland, Oregon, April 2, 1902. He was educated in the Tacoma, Washington, schools and went on in his college studies to the University of Washington, where he received the bachelor of arts degree in 1923, and the master of arts degree in 1924. Early as an undergraduate he found two interests, philosophy and psychology, that were to occupy him throughout his professional life.

At Washington Baylis studied with William Savery, whose views in ethics he shared, though in later life he was to modify them; his other teachers, Curt DuCasse and Ralph Blake, were, with Arthur Murphy, to become his colleagues in the Department of Philosophy at Brown University. He completed his graduate studies at Harvard. There C. I. Lewis was the teacher whose views most influenced him. Harvard awarded him the Sheldon Traveling Fellowship. He spent the year, 1926, in Europe, principally at Cambridge University, and on vacations bicycled through France and Germany with his wife, the former Ruth Woodruff Weage, a fellow student at the University of Washington whom he had married August 21, 1925, while still a graduate student at Harvard.

DuCasse had invited him to join the Department of Philosophy at Brown and he taught there from 1927 to 1948. His early articles, for example, "The Philosophic Functions of Emergence," reflected the interests he had developed at Washington and that were expressed in his dissertation *Creative Synthesis as a Philosophic Concept*. But stimulated by the work of C. I. Lewis and by his association with the mathematician A. A. Bennett he turned more to logic and the philosophy of logic. With Bennett he published *Formal Logic*. He was one of the founders of the Association for Symbolic Logic and one of the founding editors of the *Journal of Symbolic Logic*. He served as Secretary-Treasurer of the Association from 1936 to 1942, and as Vice-president for the period 1942–46.

He left Brown to become Chairman and Professor of Philosophy at the University of Maryland; in 1952 he joined the Department of Philosophy at Duke University. He was appointed Chairman in 1956 and served in that office until 1968. His intelligence and reputation attracted a group of very able philosophers and his warmth and capacity for friendship kept them together throughout his stay.

With Everett Hall, then chairman at the Department of Philosophy at the University of North Carolina at Chapel Hill, he helped institute a series of colloquia highly valued by both departments; there were joint seminars, and the practice was established that was to last until the death of Everett Hall of meeting regularly for philosophic discussion. His association with Everett Hall is reflected in his publication during this period of his *Ethics: Principles of Wise Choice*. But in addition to reflecting on issues in moral philosophy, during his active philosophic life he gave much thought to metaphysics and epistemology, and published numerous articles in these fields. His considerable reputation rests on these as much as anything.

It was during this period that his fellow philosophers paid him the tribute of electing him to the office of President of the Southern Society for Philosophy and Psychology, a regional association of philosophers and psychologists in the southeastern states, and electing him Vice-President for the Eastern Division of the American Philosophical Association. Among his academic honors should be listed his appointment as a Fulbright Senior Scholar, and his appointment as a Guggenheim Fellow for 1958–59.

A long list of able students can testify to the interest in philosophy he was able to evince in them: his lectures were lively, witty, and lucid. They expressed well an engaging human being. This volume of essays is an expression of admiration from some of his colleagues and friends and a tribute to him as a philosopher and human being.

Fact, Value, and Perception

Facts, Fact-correlates, and Fact-surrogates

Romane L. Clark

Indiana University

I. *Fact-correlates*

The appeal to facts is often thought to be an idle appeal. Professor Baylis did not think so. In his important 1948 article, "Facts, Propositions, Exemplification and Truth,"[1] he argued that the correspondence between a true proposition and the fact which makes it true is a species of *exemplification:* ". . . true propositions characterize facts, and . . . these facts embody or exemplify the abstract propositional meanings they make true" (p. 460). Facts are to the propositions they make true, as particulars are to the properties they instantiate.

This is a novel and exciting thesis, the larger implications of which must be set aside here. For now, there is a simple and prior question: if the truth of a proposition consists in its being exemplified by a fact which makes it true, how are we to state *this* fact, the fact that it does so? It is true, let us suppose, that Mary is making pies. It is, Baylis maintains, "the actual situation in the kitchen" which is now characterized by Mary's making pies; it is, he maintains, "the state of affairs regarding New York's buildings in its concrete actuality [which] is characterized by the Empire State Building being taller than the Woolworth Building"; "It is the actual state of affairs in my garden which will be characterized by there being a red rose there but is not now so characterized" (p. 469).

We do not now distinguish facts, situations, and states of affairs. The important thing is that, on Baylis's view, facts (situations, states of affairs) are objects of reference. They have properties, as well as exemplifying propositional meanings; they are actual, concrete; they have locations, they reside in kitchens and gardens on varying occasions. They must be, it seems evident, the objects of certain pronomial and quantificational references.

We may, presumably, give explicit formal expression to the statement

---

1. *Mind,* 57, ns, no. 228, 459–479.

that the actual situation in the kitchen is characterized by Mary's making pies:

(1) $(\exists f)[F(f) \& I(f,$ the kitchen, now$) \& E(f,$ that Mary is making pies$)]$,

Where 'F' is the predicate 'is a fact', 'I' is 'in', and 'E' is 'exemplifies'. If we construe 'that Mary is making pies is exemplified by f' as an expression of the kind of fact that f is, that f is a making of (certain) pies by Mary, then (1) perhaps may be expanded as follows:

(2) $(\exists f)[F(f) \& I(f,$ the kitchen, now$) \& M(f,$ these pies, Mary$)]$.

We read: there exists a fact in Mary's kitchen which is a making of (certain) pies by Mary.

So understood, Baylis's novel way with facts anticipated by a couple of decades the more recent, but similar, analysis of events by Donald Davidson.[2] Baylis's facts in Mary's kitchen match Davidson's events (embodying Mary's action there). In both cases, we have a reference to something which is, or which is in some way correlated with, the fact that Mary is making pies in the kitchen now. Both admit of "categorizing predications" which are truth-entailing. That is, that there is such a fact, or that such an event obtains, implies, evidently, that Mary is making pies. Now if there is a fact of the sort recorded in (1) or (2) then we ought on occasion to be able to refer directly and determinately to it. What then is the fact the existence of which satisfies the bracketed, open sentences occurring in (1) and (2) and which ensures the truth of their existential quantifications, (1) and (2) themselves? And how is reference to this fact secured?

There are a number of nominalizing transformations in English which turn a declarative sentence into a singular referring expression. To the truth that Caesar is dead there is a set of nominalizing phrases: there is the reference to the event, 'Caesar's death' (or 'the death of Caesar'); there is a reference to that fatal process, 'Caesar's dying'; there is a reference to that enduring terminal state, 'Caesar's being dead'. These are, of course, phrases with distinct references, as has often been remarked. Caesar's death occurred at a time, his dying was protracted for a time, but his being dead is neither dated nor protracted. We may think of the event, the process, and outcome as each a "fact-correlate." Each is something the existence of which is dependent upon a correlated fact, the fact that Caesar is dead. This is not to say, however, that any refer-

---

2. See his "The Logical Form of Action Sentences," *The Logic of Decision and Action,* ed. Nicholas Rescher (University of Pittsburgh Press, 1967), pp. 81–95. See, too, Davidson's contributions to Symposium II: "On Events and Event-Descriptions," *Fact and Existence,* ed. Joseph Margolis (Basil Blackwell, 1969), pp. 74–84.

ence to one of these entails that the fact-correlate exists. We say truly perhaps that Mary's marriage will be next June or has been called off. The need for categorizing predicates, like 'is a fact', ascriptions of which are truth-entailing, lies in the fact that references to fact-correlates do not by their occurrence alone support Existential Generalization.

Baylis's account appeals to nominalizations which make reference to fact-correlates. Apparently, these are mainly references to states, for 'Mary's making pies' and 'Caesar's being dead' are the kind of nominalization he seems to favor. In any case, there is a difficulty here for his "exemplificational theory of truth." For correlated with a fact though they may be, still events, states and processes are not themselves facts. And if Baylis's references are to these, then it is these apparently, and not their associated facts, which should exemplify propositions on Baylis's theory. Baylis owes us then an account of how they do so and of the relation of fact-correlates to the facts with which they are correlated. Are there states, events, processes in addition to facts? What is the relation that these have to the propositions which are made true by their correlated facts?

We are perhaps being unjustly literal. Apart from his examples, what Baylis's theorizing requires is a set of singular referring expressions for facts, those entities which make true the propositions which are true (by exemplifying them) and categorizing predicates which are truth-entailing (like 'is a fact'). We can think of the former as supplied by adding to standard logic an operator which when applied to a sentence yields a singular term. If 'P' is the sentence 'Mary is making pies', let '$[P]$' be the singular term 'the fact that Mary is making pies' (or perhaps more colloquially but less accurately, 'Mary's making pies'). And we can think of adding a special, one-place truth-entailing categorizing predicate 'P', (e.g., 'is a fact' or 'obtains'). Baylis seems to assume the following:

(3)   If $F[A]$ then A,

for any closed wff A since 'F' is truth-entailing. But if (3) is the case then it is itself a fact and we should be able to record *that*. We have then on Baylis's view

(4) $F[\text{If } F[A], \text{ then } A]$.

Presumably, we have the distribution of "fact-hood":

(5)   If $F[\text{If } A, \text{ then } B]$, then if $F[A]$ then $F[B]$.

There is a certain danger in this characterization, underdetermined as it is. For 'obtains' is reminiscent of 'is true'. If we interpret (3) through (5) syntactically, setting $[A]$ identical to the Gödel number of the sentence A, a minimally rich theory containing such principles is inconsistent.[3] This however will not be an acceptable interpretation on a theory (like Davidson's, say) in which '$[A]$' refers to a fact-correlate (an event, for example). But neither will it do as an interpretation of Baylis's theory as we now construe it with its references to facts.[4] It is clear that (3) through (5) are not for Baylis syntactical assertions, nor 'F' a number-theoretic predicate. This is clear for Baylis wishes to hold that facts exemplify many distinct propositions just as particulars exemplify many different attributes. In particular, then, '$[A] = [B]$' may well be true on Baylis's theory although 'A' and 'B' are distinct sentences. For Baylis there may be many singular referring expressions the varying references of which are values satisfying the bracketed open clauses quantified in (1) and (2). 'Mary's rolling out the dough now' might be another such reference if in fact Mary's making pies comes to that.

There is point to this for on Baylis's view one and the same completely determinate, concrete fact may make true many distinct propositions. The same fact exemplifies, and so makes true, the propositions that Mary is making pies, that she is making apple pies, that someone is in the kitchen. It is a merit of his thesis that he offers an account which explains why it is that the proposition that Caesar died slowly entails the proposition that Caesar died without invoking, ad hoc, meaning postulates as suppressed premises.

But there is also a strong temptation to deny that these apparent singular references to facts or fact-correlates are literal references. Many apparent references succumb to paraphrase:

'Caesar's dying was protracted' is to say no more, perhaps, than that Caesar died slowly. 'Mary's being here precludes John's having the guest room' is, perhaps, merely an encapsulation of the tissue of suppressed social requirements and present fact the upshot of which is recorded in the abridged inference that since Mary is here, John cannot be given the room. It is, no doubt, an article of faith that adequate paraphrases which do not contain such nominalizing phrases will always be forthcoming.[5] There is reason however to suppose that this once at least Faith and Truth coincide. For we must ask, on Baylis's theory, when a reference to a fact actually designates a fact. The naive answer is that it does so when the matching statement is true. 'Mary's making pies' designates a fact or its correlate just in case it is true that Mary is making pies.

3. See e.g. R. Montague, "Syntactical Treatments of Modality, with Corollaries on Reflexion Principles and Finite Axiomatizability," *Proc. of a Colloquium on Modal and Many-Valued Logics, Acta Philosophica Fennica*, Fasc. XVI (1963) pp. 153–167.

4. As my colleague, Nino Cocchiarella, has stressed to me. The same point was made by Professor Charles Kielkopf of Ohio State University where, in 1971, an earlier version of this paper was presented.

5. This article of faith is not shared, it seems, by Davidson. Singular causal statements typically embody ineliminable references to events, if he is right. See, e.g., his "Causal Relations," *The Journal of Philosophy*, 64, no. 21 (Nov. 9, 1967), 691–703.

It is not an idle consideration to note that we do not use, because we do not have, "simple" proper names or demonstratives for facts. Categorizing references, phrases like 'the fact that *P*' *(TFT-P)*, can be contextually eliminated in terms of simple assertions and fact-correlates: '*G(TFT-P)*' is just '*P* & *G*[*P*]'. I assume here that these last, the occurrences of fact-correlates, are replaceable by paraphrase case by case. If there are facts, they are not, given our assumption, the objects of singular reference. If they are not, then we cannot state Baylis's theory of truth. That theory, we recall, laid down something like this:

(7)   '*A*' is true iff ($\exists f$)($F(f)$ & $E(f$, the proposition that A)).

But the right-hand side of (7) only makes sense, it was argued, if there are possible singular referring expressions to replace the variable '*f*'. Facts, for Baylis, are defined as the individuals which exemplify propositions. But individuals, (even abstract ones), can be referred to.

If facts cannot be the objects of singular reference, it seems to follow that there are no facts. For, surely, anything there is can be singularly referred to. So it may be concluded that either the suppositions and suggestions that underlay the rejection of Baylis's theory must themselves be rejected, or else we must accept the consequence that there are no facts.

II. *Facts Without Fact-correlates*

It is possible, of course, consistently to maintain both that there are facts and that facts cannot be the objects of singular reference. We have merely to deny that every thing there is can be the object of singular reference. Facts, in particular, cannot be referred to in this way and yet do exist if, for example, Russell was right.[6] On this view, facts are *asserted* by statements, and facts *make true* those statements which are true. Facts, however, are not individuals and statements are not names. Ontologically, facts have a complexity that individuals do not have. (Constituents in facts are not parts of facts.) Semantically, statements are complex in their valuations in a way names are not in their interpretations. Facts, on Russell's analysis, are not named but stated.[7]

We have reasons for holding that facts are not the objects of singular reference. There remain as well independent reasons for supposing that, nevertheless, there are facts.

The point in the appeal to facts lies primarily in the logic of the notion 'makes true'. While statements cannot, on present assumptions, embody

6. See, e.g., B. Russell, *The Problems of Philosophy*, ch. XII., pp. 124–130.
7. E. W. Hall, *What Is Value?* follows Russell in this.

singular references to facts (and so do not embody references to the facts which make them true), statements do *assert* facts and facts do *make true* our true statements. It is not the case, however, that a fact which makes a statement true is necessarily a fact which the statement asserts. The non-triviality of the appeal to facts resides essentially in this, that statement and fact, although related, are not related in a one-one correspondence.

The facts of the matter, imagine, are these: John kissed Mary last night on the porch; Bill did too.

The one statement, 'Someone kissed Mary last night', is made true by each of the two facts and asserts neither. Bill accuses John: "You kissed Mary." John replies, "So I did." One fact makes true the two, nonsynony-mous, statements. Bill: "I kissed her first." John: "I kissed her first." A fact makes true just one of two statements, each made using the same sentence.

Evidently, then, facts cannot in general be identified with true proposi-tions, if true propositions are the meanings of true statements. Evidently the appeal to facts is not just an idle restatement in ontological idiom of the semantic theory of truth together with the truth-conditions for the inferences of standard logic. For one fact may make distinct statements true neither of which implies the other. And there may be no one fact which makes true each of two statements one of which implies the other.

Baylis's theory was motivated by a genuine concern. There is a speci-ficity about what there is that escapes our powers of description. We say, "John kissed Mary," and that is true. He did, on the porch last night, early in the evening, one hand petting the Irish setter, eyes open, . . . , . The dots, in a sense, are not eliminable. And facts, in a sense, really are like particulars (and unlike theoretical entities). Particulars are indefinitely describable in ever further detail. But a reference to a particular need not be an infinitely long description. So too a fact may be asserted in state-ments of ever greater complexity, but a statement need not be highly complex to assert a fact. We may, but we need not, respond to the deter-minateness of fact by contrast to the abstractness of assertion as did Baylis; we might consider facts to be a kind of individual. Be that as it may, what any theory of facts must in any case do is to provide a basis for entailments like this: John kissed Mary, last night, on the porch; there-fore, John kissed Mary. Evidently, any fact which makes true the premise makes true the conclusion. In general, an adequate account of facts should accomodate those inferences from statements with richly modified predi-cates to statements like them but with less richly modified predicates. For here, again, one and the same fact may make true more than one statement, and here again two statements of different complexity may assert the same fact (again rather as one and the same particular may be the object of varying references with varying descriptive detail).

Moreover, not every implication in the sense of standard logical theory is justified by appeal to the facts which make its component statements true. Accordingly, an adequate theory of facts is not a pale reflection of what we already have, a theory of the truth conditions for the sentences of standard logic. In particular, a fact which makes true the statement that *A*, say, may not make true the statement, *B* or not *B*, although the former implies the latter in standard logical theories. A fact, then, may make statements true none of which implies the others, and statements which do imply one another may be made true by distinct, and unrelated facts. It is, rather, to the simple theory of (first-degree) entailment that facts bring articulate semantical grounding.[8] What makes true a statement must, we usually suppose, make true any statement it entails. For the most part, what we suppose is true. What makes *A* true, makes true what *A entails* (e.g., that *A* or *B*, say). But what makes *A* true need not make true what *A implies* (*B* or not-*B*, say).

There is, then, in the lack of any simple match between statement and fact, and in the logic of predicate modifiers, and in the theory of entailment, philosophical motivation for supposing that there are facts. If we suppose that there are we require some account of the nature, identity conditions, numbers, and kinds of facts. Moreover, on present assumptions the theory must hold that the natural expressions of its own requirements are literally nonsense, for facts can only be asserted, not referred to. Apparent references to facts must somehow be systematically reconstrued. We turn now to a characterization of such an account, pausing first to consider an objection.

The objection is by now a familiar one, that there can be at most one fact. The argument (variously associated with Frege, Gödel, Church, Quine)[9] is in one version this: assume the following: that declarative sentences are complex names; that the reference of a complex name is a function of the references of its syntactically distinct parts; that only nonlogical expressions have a reference; and that logically equivalent expressions have the same reference. Let '*Fa*' and '*Gb*' be arbitrary declarative sentences which agree in truth-value. It follows then that '*Fa*' and '*Gb*' have the same reference.

(i)　$\hat{x}(Hx \ \& \ Fa) = \hat{x}(Hx)$

8. As Bas C. Van Fraassen pointed out in his important paper, "Facts and Tautological Entailments," *The Journal of Philosophy*, 66, no. 15 (Aug. 7, 1969), 477–487. His characterization of facts is slightly different there from that which follows here, but his conditions will be directly exploited in our altered characterization. (Entailments of degree greater than one are entailments which obtain between statements of entailments. The theory of first-degree entailments referred to here is not, to my knowledge, adequate to express iterated entailments.)

9. See, e.g., D. Davidson, op. cit., *Fact and Existence*, p. 77.

is logically equivalent to '*Fa*' and so, by the assumptions above, has the same reference as has '*Fa*'. But since $\hat{x}(Hx \& Fa) = \hat{x}(Hx \& Gb)$, substituting identities in (i) gives

(ii) $\hat{x}(Hx \& Gb) = \hat{x}(Hx)$

which has the same reference as (i). But (ii) is logically equivalent to

(iii)   *Gb*.

Thus (iii) has the same references as (ii), and, by the transitivity of 'same reference as', '*Fa*' has the same reference as has '*Gb*'. Hence, any two arbitrary declarative sentences which agree in truth-value have the same reference. If, in particular, a certain fact is the reference of a given true sentence, then that fact is the reference of every true sentence.

The argument, however, is not compelling. In the first place, the fact which makes true an assertion need not, for all we know, be the fact which is asserted by the assertion (even assuming for the sake of the argument that what a declarative sentence refers to is what a statement resulting from its use asserts). The argument at most shows that there is some one thing to which all sentences which agree in truth-value refer. It only proves that there is at most one fact if we also assume that what makes a sentence true is what is referred to by the sentence.

But apart from this, and more importantly, we can view the argument as a reductio of the assumptions upon which it is based. Evidently, there are two points at which we might try to break the argument by rejecting one of the underlying assumptions. We might, for instance, reject the step from (i) to (ii), turning as it does upon the assumption that the reference of a complex name is a function of the references of its syntactically distinct parts in such a fashion that substitution into it of expressions with the same reference leaves the reference of the complex name unaltered.

It is more plausible, however, to break the inference at the step from '*Fa*' to (i), or from (ii) to (iii), each turning as it does upon the assumption that logically equivalent sentences have the same reference. For why should we suppose that this is so? (iii), for instance, refers to an individual and asserts that the individual has a property. By contrast, (ii) refers to certain classes and asserts that they are identical. Why should we suppose that what makes true the assertion about the individual *b* should be the same as that which makes true the assertion about the classes? But (ii) and (iii) are logically equivalent.

We see, then, that the "one-fact argument" is not compelling but conditional upon the assumption that logically equivalent sentences have the same reference. But it was just such an assumption which a theory of facts attempts to call into question if it is to be a significant theory. A significant theory will, we recall, distinguish entailments from implications and so, a fortiori, from mutual implications. The one-fact argument, resting as it does upon its assumption about logical equivalents, begs that issue at the outset. From the perspective of the considerations which motivate the theory of facts, the argument is a reductio ad absurdum demonstration that logically equivalent assertions need not have the same references; that assuming they do leads to the unacceptable consequence that there is at most one fact.

III. *Fact-surrogates*

If, then, there are facts, and more than one of these, how many are there? And what kinds? In what can the identity conditions consist for entities which cannot be referred to?

Russell thought facts were complexes of a certain sort.[10] In the simplest cases, these consisted of particulars exemplifying qualities or properties, or standing to one another in relations. The problem, however, is this: if facts cannot be "named," i.e., if they cannot be the objects of singular reference but can only be asserted, how can we say, for instance, when the fact that makes true a certain statement is the same or different from that which makes true another statement? How can we say that this fact is *this kind* of fact, but that fact, another?

'Makes true', of course, is a metalinguistic concept. Our *discourse about* facts, as contrasted with our *assertion of* facts, is essentially metalinguistic. The logic of first-order tautological entailments, and the logic of predicate modifiers, can be explicated in a semantical metalanguage with enriched resources. These enriched resources do not quite require references to facts, though the effect must be as though this were the nature of the case. It suffices for formal purposes to consider, not a domain of facts, but a domain of fact-surrogates and to restrict our references to these. In doing this, our enriched semantics stands to facts rather as classical semantical discourse stands to properties. Just as classical semantical theory associates to each predicate a certain extension, the set of all and only those (n-tuples of) objects which have the property (relation) expressed by the predicate on a given interpretation, so, too, we associate with each sentence a certain set of fact-surrogates. In the simplest cases, these are sets of triples. The constituents of such ordered triples are the constituents of a complex, (a fact), which is asserted by a sentence on a given interpretation. It comes, together with an indication of the manner of combination of the constituents—i.e., of the fact's modality. To a sentence, '$P(a_1, \ldots, a_n)$', there will be a set of fact-surrogates of the form: $<R^*, <a_1^*, \ldots, a_n^*>, w_i>$. Here, R^* is the relation (or

10. Op. cit.

set of n-tuples) associated on a given interpretation with the predicate 'P' and each a_i^* is an individual from a given domain which is associated with each individual term, a_i. The first two elements of the triple are the constituents of the fact — that property or relation, and those individuals — which stand in the nexus of exemplification. The third member of the triple, 'w_i', is a "location" or "possible world." This index indicates the form of combination or copulation which is reflected in the verbal inflections of a sentence in our native language, which is tacit in the concatenation of terms in standard formalizations, and which is made explicit in alethic or modal tense logics, for example.

Not every atomic proposition, in the sense of standard logical theory, is logically simple in a sense important for the theory of facts. Let us call a predicate which has no predicates as parts a "core predicate." A "basic assertion," then, is one made using an atomic sentence the predicate of which is a core predicate. Intuitively, basic assertions are the simplest assertions relative to a language which are made true by the fact which they assert. Not only are nonatomic assertions not basic, neither are ones with modified predicates (like 'runs rapidly'). Presumably, there also are inferential relations which obtain among singular assertions which predicate natures, dispositions, or qualities of individuals, or which classify individuals into kinds. If so, some of these assertions will be made true by facts which they do not assert. Which predicates of a natural language are core predicates of the language, and so which assertions are basic assertions of the language, is a question which we ignore here.

Suppose now that we have at hand some classical interpretation, I, which assigns individuals of some nonempty denumerable domain, D, to the individual terms of our logic, and which assigns n-tuples of individuals of D to the core predicates. A new interpretation, I^*, assigns a set of fact-surrogates to each predicate. For complex predicates, MP, consisting of a predicate, P, and predicate modifier, M, this assignment will depend upon the kind of modifier M is together with the assignment I^* has already made to P.[11] For core predicates, P^n, I^* assigns a set of fact-surrogates of the form $<R^*, <a_1^*, \ldots, a_n^*>, w_o>$, where '$w_o$' is the "real-world" or "actuality" index and where R^* and each a_i^* are so associated by the classical interpretation, I, with a 'p^n' and with 'a_i's that '$P^n(a_1, \ldots, a_n)$' is true on the classical valuation.

A basic (hence atomic, nonmodal, present-tense) sentence is accordingly *made true* by just one fact; the fact which it may plausibly be said (to be used) to assert (on a given interpretation). Sets of fact-surrogates are associated with complex assertions in the following manner. To each sentence of the form *(P ∨ Q)*, I^* associates the set of fact-surrogates

11. See R. Clark, "Concerning the Logic of Predicate Modifiers," *Nous*, 4, no. 4, (Nov., 1970), esp. 331–332.

consisting of all members of the sets associated with P and with Q. To each sentence of the form $(P \& Q)$, I^* associates a set of pairs of fact-surrogates; these are all pairs the first member of which is a member of the set of fact-surrogates associated with P and the second member of which is a member of the set associated with Q.

Negative assertions can be viewed in various ways. We may, for instance, suppose that just as each true assertion is made true by some fact so too each false assertion is *made false* by some fact, this of course being also a fact which makes true the true negation of the false assertion. Or we may suppose that a false assertion is false just in case there is no fact which makes it true.

We shall not argue here the question of whether or not there exist (so-called) "negative facts." The simplest course (although not necessarily the most defensible course philosophically), seems to be this.[12] Let I^* assign to each negation of a basic assertion a set of fact-surrogates whose sole member is $<\bar{R}^*, <a_1, \ldots, a_n>, w_o>$, where $\bar{R}^*$ is the complement of R^*. Thus, the fact which makes the negation, $-A$, of the basic assertion, A, true is also the fact which makes A itself false. In general, the set of fact-surrogates associated with any true negation of the form $-A$ may be said to be the "Falsity Set" of A.

I^* associates with each sentence of the form $(x)Px$ the set of all and only those (perhaps infinite) n-tuples consisting of one member from each of the sets associated by I^* with each sentence of the form Pa_i, where 'a_i' occurs free in 'P' at each free occurrence of 'x' in 'Px'.

(Readers may recall that Russell at one point (in the *Lectures on Logical Atomism*) argued that we require "general facts" to make sentences of the form $(x)P$ true, since we require not only that Pa_i, for each a_i, but also that no individuals have been left out, — that we have covered them all. Presumably, Russell confused conditions for knowing the truth of assertions of the form $(x)P$ with conditions for their being true.)

Finally, to each sentence of the form $\ulcorner P$, I^* associates the set of all and only those n-tuples consisting of one member from each of the sets associated by I^* with P for each w_i.

A sentence, A, is true on an interpretation, I^*, just in case the "Truth Set" of A, the set of fact-surrogates associated by I with A, is not empty. Each member of the Truth Set of an assertion, A, *makes A true*.

Enough has been said now to establish contact with other discussions, and with our earlier questions, concerning facts. We have borrowed, in our characterization of fact surrogates, enough of van Fraassen's conditions to provide immediate access to his account of facts and of tautological entailments. The interested reader may easily make the accommodation. We have as immediate consequences many of the motivating

12. Here, too, we follow van Fraassen, op. cit., esp. p. 484.

features which originally suggested that an appeal to facts need not be an idle appeal. Evidently, facts which belong to the Truth Set of an assertion need not be the facts which (on any intuitive understanding) the assertion states. (Thus, a disjunction is made true by any member of the Truth Set of one of its disjuncts. An existential assertion is made true by any "instantiation" occurring in its Truth Set.) And a fact which makes true an assertion may not make true some assertion *implied* by it.

Similarly, enough has been said to make contact with a theory of predicate modifiers, based on a semantics of fact-surrogates, which ensures (as extant theories of first-order logic have failed to do) that entailments from certain rich characterizations of matters of fact to more austere statements of these same facts are valid.[13] (Thus, it follows on a semantics like that outlined, that 'John kissed Mary, last night, on the porch' entails 'John kissed Mary'.)

We are in a position now to comment upon the questions which initiated this final section of our paper. These questions are, given the present view of facts, amenable to rather trivial, and pretty immediate answers.

How many facts are there? That is, perhaps, in the last analysis not a trivial question. But we can say at least how many facts a given theory is committed to there being. For example, if on a given theory, there is a domain of discourse with a denumerable but infinite number of individuals, then, on that theory, there must be at least nondenumerably many facts. For the set of fact-surrogates is the set of all those distinct triples the first member of which is a set of n-tuples of members of the domain. And the power set of the set of all sets of n-tuples of the domain is, given a denumerably infinite domain, nondenumerable. So there must be nondenumerably many fact-surrogates. Since there must be, on the theory, as many facts as surrogates, there must be, on the theory, nondenumerably many facts. In such a case, there are more facts than can ever be separately, individually, asserted. (If so, facts cannot, on such a theory, be identified with the true propositions expressed by assertions.)

Although there may be on a given theory many facts, there is, in a sense, only one *kind* of fact. There are no special truth-functional or general facts corresponding to truth-functionally complex or quantified statements. These last, we have seen, are made true by one or more of the facts which make true certain basic assertions as well. A fact simply is the exemplification of a property (or ordered instantiation of a relation) by an individual (or n-tuple of individuals). But although there is only one kind of fact, there are as many species of fact as there are distinct types of property or relation, or distinct kinds of individuals, or distinct modes of exemplification. There are, then, in these further senses, qualitative and relational facts; physical and mental, and phenomenological

13. Clark, op. cit.

facts. And there are possible-, tense-, deontic- and normative-facts. Distinct species of fact match then distinctions in the types of constituents which comprise facts, and match the distinct manners of their combination. Copula modifiers (e.g., of tense, possibility, or of obligation) reflect or determine distinct styles or modes of exemplification. One may say if he chooses, that there are modal facts, the facts relations among which modal logics articulate; that is, the facts which make true, true tensed, modal, and deontic assertions. But there are in this sense relational and psychical and other facts as well. Accordingly, there are no dramatically different kinds of fact whose presence is reflected in our language by the occurrence of copula modifiers. Rather, the dramatic case is (or appears to be), reflected in the existence of the distinct moods. For if we resist the temptation to conflate the moods with modals (if, that is, we insist on the difference between the forms of the copula and the copula modifiers), and if the several moods do not collapse into expressions of some single, basic mood form, then there are indeed logically distinct kinds of sentential form. If so, it might be thought that there are also distinct kinds of natural complexes to which they correspond.

It is reasonable, it seems, to insist that the moods of speech should be sharply distinguished from the modalities. (For example, there are speech acts which go with the "genuine" moods of speech but not with the "genuine" modals—we state, query or command something, but we do not necessitate or future it.) It also is reasonable, it seems, to suppose that some moods are not basic but are eliminable given the other moods and modal resources. (Thus, Lennart Åqvist construes interrogatives as disguised imperatives, roughly, as being requests for information.)[14]

Reasonable or not, it is not important to argue these matters here. For what is important here is this: whether or not the other moods are eliminable, or are identified with modals, the indicative mood has a primary status upon which the other speech moods are logically parasitic. "Make it the case that," "Is it the case that," "Would that it were the case that," all presuppose the significance of "It is the case that." Each is such that the truth conditions of any sentence to which they are meaningfully prefixed are also the satisfaction conditions of the resulting sentence. To know in the doing of what obedience to a command consists, or to know in what the information which would satisfy a query consists, is to know that which can be asserted in a declarative assertion. It is reasonable, then, to suppose that an ontology which is rich enough to provide the resources required to explicate the conditions under which declaratives

14. *A New Approach to the Logical Theory of Interrogatives* (Uppsala, 1965). The fundamental mistake which remains (on the present view of things) rests in his going on to treat imperatives as modalized statements. In fact, Åqvist frequently gives these a deontic reading. But surely we must distinguish the imperative, the vehicle by which we issue commands, from deontic assertions which record the obligations under which an agent may lie.

are (made) true, is also rich enough to characterize the conditions under which imperatives or questions are fulfilled, and to do so, without appeal to further entities. In this sense, then, it is plausible to think that there is only one kind of fact, although there may be many species of that kind.

A terminological remark together with a nonterminological point should be made here. Not all facts, as these have been characterized in this paper, exist or obtain. It may seem, or be, dissembling to call possible, but nonactual, complexes "facts." We can of course then reserve "fact" for those complexes which obtain if we like; perhaps "state of affairs" can be used instead to cover both facts and those complexes which do not obtain. The nonterminological point is that there are possible but nonactual states of affairs. This is of course a consequence of the characterization given here of facts. People of varying ontological persuasions may be exercised by this consequence. But however they parse their ontological commitments, every adequate theory will have to give expression to the fact that it was, but is not now, the case that Hoover is President (just as Hoover did, but does not now, exist). Similarly, each such theory must find a place for the truths that some bits of fiction might have been, although they are not, true descriptions of the actual world (just as it is true that some fictional characters indeed might have existed, although they do not exist).

These raise questions of modality which must be set aside here. The interested reader will have to choose up sides with respect to the alternatives discussed in the burgeoning literature on modality. We merely remark, quite ingenuously, that although there are states of affairs which are not actual, to say this is precisely to say that there are no such states of affairs. It is to say what would have made certain assertions true, if the facts had been different. In any case, these questions of modality spill over into discussions of the identity of facts as well.

In one sense, we immediately, and trivially, have identity conditions for states of affairs. The identity conditions of fact-surrogates are already at hand, since these are merely ordered triples. It is an easy step to say that the matching complexes or states of affairs are, similarly, the same when they consist of the same constituents in the same manner of combination. The further questions concerning the identity, and identifying conditions, of these constituents are of course not questions with respect to which a theory of facts imposes any special conditions nor presupposes any special implications. (Two basic assertions, say of the forms 'Fa' and 'Gb' may be said to be made true by the same fact just in case they are true, 'a' and 'b' designate the same individual, and to be F is to be G, and conversely. The identity of a and b need not, of course, be necessary nor need 'F' and 'G' be synonymous. Relative to some w_i, to be F is to be

G, and conversely, I think, just in case that, for any individual term, i, and predicate modifier, M, 'MFi' is true if and only if 'MGi' is.)

The modal spill-over comes in the trans-world identification of states of affairs, if this is possible. Whereas the one-world identity of facts seems a trivial matter, there remains the urge to identify states of affairs "across worlds." And this seems a deep, nontrivial matter presupposing as it does the identity of individuals across worlds, and of properties and relations with varying patterns of exemplifications. But I suspect that the right response is to deny that facts ever are literally the same "across distinct worlds." Fact-surrogates, whose third members are different indices, are of course, distinct surrogates. Similarly, states of affairs the direct assertion of which involves, say, different temporal modifications or inflections of the copula are different states of affairs. Past and future states of affairs are not the same states of affairs however similar they may otherwise be in their constituents. In general, what ought to be or might be is distinct from what is or was. In general, a state of affairs which "obtains in one possible, but nonactual world" is distinct from any other which "obtains in any other distinct possible world" although the same individuals and properties may occur in each.

The Real Subject-Predicate Asymmetry

John Heintz

The University of Calgary

To take a concrete example, let us suppose that within a given specious present we are aware of two sense-data, a large blue patch and a small red patch. . . . We know with certainty in this case that the blue patch is larger than the red one. . . . We are not aware merely of two patches and conjunctively added to them a relation. . . . The complex whole of the relation holding between its terms is a fact, a particular fact, if you like, but not a particular in the sense of a substance, like either of the patches.[1]

We cannot avoid admitting facts about particulars as well as particulars, because to describe a particular by means of an adjective is simply one way of saying that the particular has, in the sense of exemplifies, the character signified by that adjective.[2]

Facts are entities in relation. At the lowest level they are relations among particulars such as one patch or building being larger than another, or they are relations of exemplification between the particulars and the characters which characterize them, as for example a given patch being red.[3]

In these passages, as elsewhere, Professor Baylis succeeds in compressing a whole metaphysic into a few sentences. Certain features stand out: sense-data, certainty, facts, characters, relations, exemplification, direct awareness. My concern here is with a tension generated by Professor Baylis's differing treatments of characters and relations. In the clearly relational fact, the blue patch being larger than the red one, the role of the patches is clearly distinguished from that of the relation; the relation is not "conjunctively added" as a third term, but "holds" between the two terms to create a fact. By contrast, in the simple fact of the patch

1. C. A. Baylis, "Facts, Propositions, Exemplification and Truth," *Mind,* ns 57 (1948), 461.
2. Ibid., 461–462.
3. Ibid., 462.

being red, redness is treated as a term, like one of the patches in the relational fact, and redness is tied to the patch by the relation of exemplification.[4]

Professor Baylis seems to acknowledge that a fact is more than a mere collection of objects, and picks out in each fact a relation which binds the objects together.[5] Where the fact corresponds to a relational sentence, the relational expression is said to signify the tie that binds. Where the sentence is of the noun-copula-adjective variety, the relation of exemplification is invoked. The tension arises with Professor Baylis's later assimilation of relations to characters—abstract entities which are exemplified—for then there is one relation too many.[6] If *being taller than* binds the Empire State Building and the Woolworth Building, where does exemplification come in? If, on the other hand, 'exemplification' is just a name for the binding job which the relation achieves, what does the real binding in the fact of the patch being red?

What *are* characters (and relations) like? *Do* they enter into relations of exemplification? *Is* this the correct way to understand simple fact-stating sentences? Frege, whom Professor Baylis cites on the first and last pages of the paper under discussion, would have answered "No" to the last two. According to Frege, every simple sentence contains expression of two kinds, complete and incomplete, the former signifying the terms or objects, the latter signifying "concepts," rather like what Professor Baylis has been calling "relations," the incomplete entities which do the binding and which themselves can never be terms of relations. Thus Frege does not see

This patch is red.

and

Redness is exemplified by this patch.

as two ways of saying the same thing. What 'red' signifies in the first is an incomplete entity; what 'redness' signifies in the second is complete, an object, and hence entirely distinct.[7]

F. P. Ramsey took the opposite view. According to him, the two sentences make the same claim, express the same proposition, state the same fact. The occurrence of the word 'exemplifies', like the difference between

4. Ibid., 460–462, 476–477.

5. Compare E. W. Hall, *What is Value?* (London, 1952), ch. IV; although agreeing on this point and on the existence of facts, Professors Baylis and Hall had a long-standing disagreement, partly documented in the chapter noted, over whether facts could be named or not.

6. Baylis, op. cit., 468.

7. The *locus classicus* is his paper "On Concept and Object" translated in P. Geach and M. Black, ed., *Translations from the Writings of Gottlob Frege* (Oxford, 1952), 42–55.

'red' and 'redness' is a mere convention dictated by grammar and without ontological significance.[8] More recently, W. V. O. Quine has, to some degree, followed Frege,[9] and P. F. Strawson has taken a view on the Ramsey side rather like that of Professor Baylis, admitting that characters are generally introduced in their predicative role, but insisting that they may also be objects of singular reference, terms in relations. (He differs from Professor Baylis in calling exemplification a "non-relational tie" rather than treating it as a full-fledged relation.)[10] In spite of these disagreements, it does seem that a sentence must be more than a list of names and that the asymmetry between parts of sentences suggests an asymmetry between the kinds of entities signified by the several parts of sentences. Can anything more be said about the nature of this asymmetry? Can its existence be demonstrated? Not surprisingly, answering either of these questions requires answering both, and what follows is an attempt at another answer.

I

Suppose that particulars and their characters are indeed symmetrical from a logical point of view. Suppose as a consequence that the names of particulars and the predicate-expressions which signify characteristics of these particulars are likewise logically symmetrical. Then any truth about names must have its reflection in a truth about predicates. Quine has claimed that names can be eliminated from descriptive discourse and, more dramatically, that individual variables, the pronomial proxies for names, can also be done away with.[11] A subject-predicate *symmetry* thesis, entailing that what's good for names is good for predicates, suggests that predicates and predicate-variables should be equally eliminable. So I once thought.[12] This is how it went:

Quine starts with a typical first-order language. Names (such as 'Socrates') are traded in for predicates purportedly true of just the named individual ('socratizes'), and singular predications are interpreted via the theory of descriptions ('Socrates is snub-nosed' becoming 'The socratizer is snub-nosed'). The result is a first-order language without individual constants. Universal quantifiers are eliminated in favor of existentials by

8. F. P. Ramsey, *Foundations of Mathematics,* ed. R. B. Braithwaite (London, 1931), 116–117.

9. W. V. Quine, *Methods of Logic* (New York, 1955), 206–227.

10. P. F. Strawson, *Individuals* (London, 1959), ch. V and VI.

11. W. V. Quine, "Variable Explained Away," *Proceedings of the American Philosophical Society,* 104 (1960), 343–347.

12. John Heintz, "Identity, Quantification and Predicables," *Logique et Analyse,* 11 (1968), 390–402.

the familiar equivalences, and truth-functional connectives are replaced by their equivalents in terms of conjunction and negation. The elimination of variables then proceeds by successively replacing the negation, conjunction and existential quantification operators on well-formed formulas with operators on predicates. Thus '−Fx' becomes '(Neg F)x', 'Px & Qy' becomes '(PXQ)xy', and '(∃x)Fx' becomes '(Der F)'.[13]

How it (supposedly) goes for predicates is this. Imagine a language with individual names, predicate variables, quantification over predicate variables, and the usual truth-functional operations on well-formed formulas. The elimination of predicate variables is carried out by replacements mirroring Quine's: '−F(a)' becomes 'F(nug(a))', 'F(a) & G(b)' becomes 'FG((a)*(b))', '(∃F)F(a)' becomes 'dur(a)'.[14] And why not?

Some of the objections considered below were raised by several helpful, if discouraging, commentators, especially Nuel D. Belnap, Jr., and Paul Benacerraf. My initial replies, though correct in the context outlined above, nonetheless reveal a fundamental underlying difficulty which both exposes what subject-predicate asymmetry amounts to, and constitutes the principal argument that such asymmetry is an integral part of our conceptual framework.

II

The objections come to this: predicates can be sensibly negated, subjects cannot. On this there is nearly universal agreement. The issue is joined over the reasons why.

Admitting negated individual constants, it is claimed, leads to paradox. N. L. Wilson derived this result in his *Concept of Language*,[15] and P. T. Geach subsequently employed essentially the same argument in his *Reference and Generality*.[16] Informally, the argument goes like this: It is not the case that Socrates is both snub-nosed and not snub-nosed. Therefore the negation of Socrates, nug-Socrates, is *both* snub-nosed and not snub-nosed, a manifest contradiction. Formally, the argument proceeds in this way: Let 'Q(x)' be a defined predicate:

(D) $Q(x) \equiv (P(x) \,\&\, -P(x))$

Where 's' represents 'Socrates', we have:

$-(P(s) \,\&\, -P(s))$

13. Quine, op. cit., 344–345.
14. Heintz, op. cit., 393–395; in both versions, mine and Quine's, inversion operators and a reflexivity operator are necessary to turn the trick, but the details are not germane here.
15. N. L. Wilson, *Concept of Language* (Toronto, 1959), 56–57.
16. P. T. Geach, *Reference and Generality* (Ithaca, 1962), 31–33.

which is equivalent by (D) to

–Q(s).

The latter may be rewritten on our scheme as

Q(nug(s))

which expands by (D) to

P(nug(s)) & –P(nug(s)).

Of course, as Wilson pointed out in his book, and Robert Grimm demonstrated in response to Geach,[17] the argument turns on admitting 'Q(x)' as a defined predicate interchangeable at will with 'P(x) & –P(x)' regardless of context. Wilson concludes that neither defined individuals nor defined properties should be admitted (in the sense of allowing defined individual or predicate constants to replace variables), since to admit both leads to contradiction, and no sound principle justifies admitting one but not the other. Grimm's arguments, directed against Geach's particular theses concerning naming and predicating, are more elaborate, but make essentially the same point. Geach disagrees, replying that "the ordinary calculus of predicables is a logically sound theory," "it is an integral part of this calculus that negations and conjunctions of predicables are themselves treated as predicables," and finally that "one *needs* only a syntactically simple name to name a thing, but one may surely *need* a complex predicate to describe it."[18] The reply seems empty. One often *does* need a complex name to name something, say the *n*th term of a series, Henry VIII, or an object with which one's audience is unacquainted. One *may* of course use a simple, non-complex predicate to describe it.

More importantly, one often uses a version of first-order logic in which there are no defined predicate constants. In such a formulation the paradox does not arise. Indeed, the paradox can be avoided while permitting such defined predicates by adopting this restriction:

(R) Rewrite each sentence in primitive notation before employing operators on individual constants.

The restriction prohibits the move from

–Q(s)

to

Q(nug(s)).

17. *Analysis,* 26 (1966), 138–146.
18. Ibid., 146.

Permissible moves would include

> −Q(s)
> −(P(s) & −P(s))
> −(P(s) & P(nug(s)))
> −PP((s)*(nug(s)))
> −P(ruf((s)*(nug(s))))
> P(nug(ruf((s)*(nug(s))))).

None of these lines expresses a contradiction.

To modify one of Grimm's points: either the complex predicate one needs to describe an object is definable in the manner of 'Q(x)', in which case it can be replaced harmlessly by its definition, or such a predicate cannot be defined in the manner of 'Q(x)' in which case the contradiction cannot be derived at all.[19]

The point can be made semantically. Truth-conditions for the predicate-calculus are often expressed by first choosing a domain, then assigning elements of the domain to the individual constants and subsets and sets of ordered n-tuples of members of the domain to the monadic and n-adic predicate letters, respectively.[20] Semantics for a negated individual constant can then be expressed in these terms:

'F(nug(a))' is assigned T iff 'F(a)' is assigned F.

This rule mirrors the more familiar

'−F(a)' is assigned T iff 'F(a)' is assigned F.

and defined predicates may be dealt with in similar fashion without increasing the number of sets assigned to constants:

'(Neg F)a' is assigned T iff 'F(a)' is assigned F.

No new objects or classes need be introduced as semantic correlates of defined subjects *or* defined predicates. A sound system will remain sound with the addition of complex defined subject and predicate expressions, provided the defined terms are added with sufficient care.

III

The situation with respect to Wilson's paradox may be clarified by considering the rules of inference for a functional calculus which (unlike Quine's and mine) includes quantification over both individual and predi-

---

19. Grimm, op. cit., 141.
20. A familiar version is given in Benson Mates, *Elementary Logic*, 2nd edition (New York, 1972), ch. 4.

cate variables. One such is Leon Henkin's F^*.[21] The rules of inference for F^* are *modus ponens* and universal generalization. There are axioms sufficient to generate all the tautologies of the propositional calculus. There are in addition

(i) $(a)(A \supset B) \supset (A \supset (a)B)$ where a is any (individual or predicate) variable not free in A, and

(ii) $(a)A \supset S'{}^{a}_{b}A|$ where b is any variable or constant of the same type as a, a is a variable such that no free occurrence of a in A is in a part of the form $(b)C$, and $S'{}^{a}_{b}A|$ is the result of replacing each free occurrence of a in A by b.[22]

This system is consistent and complete with respect to the interpretation sketched at the end of the last section. It is, however, a very weak system, lacking as a theorem the intuitively valid

(1) $(\exists x)(\exists G)G(x)$.[23]

(Of course, as long as one is willing to interpret each monadic predicate as signifying the empty set, (1) will remain false; and as long as such an interpretation is included among the ones possible, (1) will remain not valid.)

Adding complex defined predicates as substituends for predicate variables would yield (1) as a theorem, and indeed amounts to adding an abstraction axiom equivalent to Henkin's

(iv) $(\exists c)(a_1) \ldots (a_n)(c(a_1, \ldots, a_n) \equiv B)$ where B is any wff, $a_1, \ldots, a_n$ are any distinct individual variables and c is any n-adic predicate variable not occurring freely in B.[24]

(iv) amounts to asserting that there is a predicable entity corresponding to each condition on individuals. The analogous axiom, equivalent to guaranteeing an individual corresponding to each complex defined individual constant, would be

21. Leon Henkin, "Banishing the Rule of Substitution for Functional Variables," *The Journal of Symbolic Logic*, 18 (1953), 201–208. I am specially grateful to Hughes Leblanc for directing my attention to this paper, which has clarified a number of confusions present in an earlier draft.

22. Ibid., 202. I have changed Henkin's *fraktur* alphabet for typographical convenience; the words are his.

23. Ibid., 202.

24. Ibid., 203.

(iv!) $(\exists a)(f_1) \ldots (f_n)(f_1 \ldots f_n(a) \equiv B)$ where B is any wff, $f_1, \ldots, f_n$ are any distinct predicate variables, and a is any individual variable not occurring freely in B.

(Note here that individual variables going proxy for complex defined individual constants will, like those constants, often be polyadic! For those who like to think of variables as formal counterparts of pronouns, a dyadic variable might correspond to the use of 'they' when, having previously identified Jane and Eleanor, one says that they are blond and bald, respectively.)

(iv) and (iv!) together will yield contradiction. Either alone will not. The point here is to highlight the fact that introducing complex defined constants, substitutable for variables, is tantamount to introducing abstraction axioms, guaranteeing that there is an entity of the appropriate sort (individual or predicable) corresponding to each complex condition on entities of the other sort. Is there any reason to adopt one of (iv) or (iv!) rather than the other? Is there any inherent reason for rejecting one of them?

IV

A generous reader will perhaps not attempt to answer these questions with thoughts about set theory and its utility for mathematics, at least not just yet. These have their place in this story, but it is in the next section. The reason is that a thousand more "paradoxes" can be generated without the introduction of defined predicates or the use of the axiom schema (iv). Recall that 'F(nug(a))' will be true, on our account, just in case '−F(a)' is true. A Few facts about Socrates:

(2) Socrates was *not* born in Pakistan.
(3) Socrates was *not* born in Ireland.
(4) Socrates was not more than 8 feet tall.
(5) Socrates was not less than 3 feet tall.
(6) Socrates was not born in 1900 A.D.
(7) Socrates did not die in 1800 A.D.

Hence:

nug(Socrates) was born in Pakistan and in Ireland.
nug(Socrates) was more than 8 feet tall and less than 3 feet tall.
nug(Socrates) was born in 1900 A.D. and nug(Socrates) died in 1800 A.D.

Things get worse. nug(Socrates) was a horse without a heart, for Socrates was not a horse but did have a heart. nug(Socrates) is an electron with a mass of 18 pounds, a bicyclist with no legs, a manx cat with a tail, and so on. There is hardly a generalization which nug(Socrates) fails to violate.[25]

Resolute commitment to a symmetry thesis can produce this lame response: when Quine eliminates singular terms and singular term variables, he does so in a system which forbids quantification over the predicate place. Elimination of predicates and predicate term variables is thus possible under precisely analogous conditions forbidding quantification over the subject place. Though true that nug(Socrates) is a horse without a heart, nug(Socrates) does not violate the generalization that all horses have hearts, for that generalization cannot be expressed. Such a response is cold comfort, even to a hardened symmetry theorist, since it purchases symmetry at the price of science.

Without reflecting on the nature either of individuals or predicable entities, without looking into the specific semantic roles of subjects or predicates, we are faced with a fundamental feature of language which conflicts with the notion of negated individual constants: language is used to express generalizations, regularities in the world, without which we could not organize our experience or state the results of science.

The real reason why there can be no negative individuals, and why axiom schema (iv!) must be rejected, is that if there really were negative individuals (guaranteed by the existence axioms corresponding to instances of (iv!) with B replaced by the formal counterparts of (1) through (7) and so on), then some horses would not have hearts, some people would be born after they die, and some electrons would weigh 18 pounds and sing tenor at the Met. We know as a matter of fact that none of these things is so. And so we know, from the possibility of there being regularities in nature, that negative individuals, constructible from elements in our domain of discourse, are impossible.

V

We have answered the question "Is there any reason for rejecting either (iv) or (iv!)?" (iv!) indeed must go. To establish a genuine subject-predicate asymmetry on this basis, however, it is necessary to show that (iv) *can* be accepted consistently.

A *model* for F^{**}, which contains (iv), is "a sequence $(K_0, K_1, \ldots, K_n, \ldots)$ such that K_0 is an arbitrary (non-empty) set, K_1 is an arbitrary (non-empty) class of subsets of K_0, and for $n > 1$, K_n is an arbitrary (non-empty) family of n-ary relations on K_0 (i.e. the elements of K_n (if

---

25. I am treating each of the predicate phrases here as monadic.

any) are ordered n-tuples of elements of K_0)."[26] Consider then a generalization

(8) $(x)(F(x) \supset G(x))$.

The relevant instance of (iv) will be

(9) $(\exists H)(x)(H(x) \equiv (F(x) \supset G(x)))$.

(8) and (9) together yield

(10) $(\exists H)(x)(H(x)$.

(10) will be true just in case K_0 is a member of K_1, that is when the model contains the universal set of its domain. (iv) just amounts to requiring that the universal set exist when generalizations are true, a consistent requirement.

VI

It might be thought that a different but fundamental subject-predicate asymmetry was overlooked at the outset. Quine supposes that each individual name may be replaced by a simple predicate true of just the individual purportedly named by the name. A symmetricist must then argue that each predicate may be replaced by a simple name which only that one predicate may be truly concatenated with. Here, surely, one finds a difference. For to each individual there corresponds its unit set, the appropriate member of K_1 to assign the new predicate. Where on earth would one find an individual which belonged to just one class, not to its union with any other, and not to the universal set or the domain? The one-classed individual is certainly a contradiction in terms. The short way with this objection is to point out that on F^* there is no paradox. The objection assumes that F^{**} or its equivalent must be the correct logic to employ. It is true that if one does assume a set theory then one will have unit sets, but set theory, however convenient, is not the only way to do semantics.

If one turns from set-theoretic considerations to the characters of individuals with which the paper began, the question becomes, "Is there for each individual a unique character which it alone exemplifies?" The way to answer this may be to determine which theory to adopt. If (iv) is included then for each constant 'a' there will be this instance

$(\exists H)(x)(H(x) \equiv x = a)$.

26. Henkin, p. 206.

VII

The fundamental difference between subjects and predicates is that we employ predicates in expressing generalizations. So some operations on subjects are prohibited. Concerns about classes, unit sets and abstraction principles are variations on that theme. Negation is an operation on predicates which *can* yield new ones. What of a higher-order calculus, where predicates of individuals may have higher-order predicates attached to them? Even there the difference between subject and predicate recurs. For '(Neg F)' is the predicative negation of 'F', but it will not be the "nugation" of 'F' as subject for higher-order predicates. For let 'ϕ' be a predicate true of all characters of individuals. Then '$\phi(F)$' will be true and '$\phi(\text{Neg } F)$' will be true as well. But '$\phi(\text{nug}(F))$' must be false.[27]

27. I am grateful to the National Endowment for the Humanities for a summer study fellowship during which some of the ideas in this paper were developed, and to Bedford College, London, its librarian Mr. R. Patterson, and its Philosophy Department, who shared their very pleasant surroundings with me during the term of that fellowship. A version of this paper was read to the Canadian Philosophical Association meeting in Montreal, June, 1972. I am grateful to Robert Binkley for his comments at that time, which I have tried to account for in the present version.

'All Men Are Mortal'

Erik Stenius
University of Helsinki

1. In Leibniz's logical writings the approach to Aristotelian syllogistics is predominantly intensional. A statement of the form

(1)   All men are mortal

is in most of his writings symbolized in the form

(2) $H = XM$,

that is, we arrive at the concept of a man (H) by adding some characteristics (X) to the concept of mortality (M).[1] Sometimes it is also written in the (equivalent) form

(2′) $H = HM$,

which means that the concept of a man is the same concept as the concept of being both a man and mortal (OFI, p. 306).

An affirmative particular statement like "Some men are wise" is symbolized as

(3) $XH = YW$,

which may be interpreted as saying that we arrive at the same (non-contradictory) concept by adding certain characteristics to the concept of a man as by adding certain other characteristics to the concept of wisdom. The other Aristotelian basic forms of statement are formalized in a corresponding way. In this paper, however, I am only interested in statements of the form (1).

2. It has been pointed out that an intensional interpretation of universal statements applies only when these statements are analytic. The statement that we arrive at the concept of a man by adding certain characteristics to the concept of mortality can be true only if, like some stoics,

---

1. Cf., for instance, Leibniz, OFI, pp. 57, 59, 233, 301, 396. For the interpretation of this formula, see Leibniz, OFI, pp. 52–53, LP, pp. 20–21. A good survey of Leibniz's different notations is found in Leibniz, FL, pp. 524ff. Throughout this paper my references to books and articles are abbreviated in a way which should be obvious from the list of references.

we regard mortality as a defining characteristic of man. It is significant that Leibniz did not, as a rule, use (1) as an example of a universal affirmative statement but the statement "All men are animals," which people at Leibniz's time certainly would have conceived of as analytic. If (1) is not taken as analytic, in a sense (cf., however, below, section 7), it cannot be regarded as a statement dealing only with the concepts of a man and mortality but also as referring to the world, to extensions.

3. This may be an argument for saying, like Couturat, that only an extensional approach to syllogistics is really possible.[2] However, a *purely* extensional approach to syllogistics turns out to run into the same difficulty as the purely intensional approach, since it tends also to making all true universal statements strictly tautological. My argument for saying this is as follows. According to a purely extensional view, (1) is logically equivalent to

(4)   The set of all men is included in the set of all mortals

or formally

(4') $S_H \subseteq S_M$,

where "S_H" denotes the set of all men and "S_M" the set of all mortals.

Now a set is uniquely determined by its elements. If (1) is logically equivalent to (4) it is also logically equivalent not only to

(5)   The set of all featherless bipeds is included in the set of all mortals,

but also to, for instance,

(6)   The set of Adam and all his descendants is included in the set of all terrestial living creatures.

(taking the teachings of the Bible for granted), or any statement of the form

(7) $S_1 \subseteq S_2$,

where, as a matter of fact, $S_H = S_1$, and $S_M = S_2$.

Let us for the sake of simplicity assume that the set of all men from Adam until the Last Judgment is finite and that the set of all mortals is also finite. Then one way of defining the sets S_H and S_M is by "enumeration" of their elements, that is, we define:

2. This is not the argument on which Couturat bases his opinion. He thinks that an intensional calculus is formally impossible (Cf. LL, pp. 24, 386f.). The same seems to be the attitude of Parkinson (Leibniz, LP. pp. xl, lx). However, a syllogistic calculus can formally be carried out as elegantly as an extensional class calculus – see Kauppi, ETB.

(8)

    (a) $S_H = \{a_1, a_2, \ldots, a_m\}$,

    (b) $S_M = \{b_1, b_2, \ldots, b_n\}$.

Now what is stated by (4′) is that any a_i is identical with some b_j. This, however, may be formalized in the following way: For any $i(1 \leqslant i \leqslant m)$ a_i is identical with some b_j $(1 \leqslant j \leqslant n)$, that is, the disjunction

(9) $D_i =_{df} a_i = b_1 \vee a_i = b_2 \vee \ldots \vee a_i = b_n$

is true for every a_i, or in other words: (4′) is equivalent to

(10) $D_1 \,\&\, D_2 \ldots \,\&\, D_m.$

However it is at least plausible to regard a statement of the form

(11) $a = b$

as tautological if it is true (and contradictory if it is false). But then (10) is also tautological if it is true, and according to the purely extensional view (1) is logically equivalent with (10). So if (1) is true it must on the purely extensional view be a tautology; otherwise it is contradictory.

    Incidentally, Leibniz in the fragment *Mathesis Rationis* (A Mathematics of Reason), which is built on an extensional basis, and which Couturat considers "the most precise and complete" Leibnizian exposition of the rules of syllogism (LL, p. 24), gives the following formulation of the "universal affirmative": "When I say 'Every A is B', I understand that any one of those which are called A is the same as some one of those which are called B." (OFI, p. 193, translated by Parkinson in LP, p. 95.) This formulation strongly reminds one of (10).

    4. Frege was strongly opposed to the conception of a statement of the form (1) as the statement of an inclusion between sets.[3] Frege was presumably the first to conceive of such a statement in the modern way as an implication statement, which is true 'for all values' of a general variable "x," and which, accordingly (by modernizing Frege's notation) can be written in the form[4]

(12) $(x)(H(x) \supset M(x)).$

This way of interpreting (1) avoids the difficulty of its tending to lapse into a tautology. Now logicians, who claim to take a purely "extensional" view of logic, seem to take (12) as consistent with this view. But in fact (12) is not purely extensional, but rather a combination of the extensional and intensional view. On the one hand it is *extensional,* since the variables

---

3. See, for instance, his criticism of Schröder, TPW, pp. 89ff.
4. See his *Begriffsschrift* (1879), sec. 11, TPW, pp. 16ff.

of the quantifier refer to individuals; on the other hand it contains the predicate symbols "$H(x)$" and "$M(x)$," which—whatever some logicians may say—refer to *intensions*. Statement (12) will not be considered as stating the same thing as another statement of the same form, say,

(12a) $(x)(H'(x) \supset M'(x))$,

only because, as a matter of fact, H has the same extension as H' and M has the same extension as M', that is, only because, as a matter of fact,

$$
(12b) \begin{cases} (x)(H(x) \equiv H'(x)) \\ \\ (x)(M(x) \equiv M'(x)). \end{cases}
$$

In order for us to be able to infer from the statements (12b) to the *logical* equivalence between (12) and (12a), we must assume not only that statements (12b) are true, but that they themselves are logical equivalences, which means that H has the same *intension* as H', and M the same intension as M'.

5. So logicians who think that (12) is purely extensional are mistaken. I think my arguments show that a purely extensional view on logic cannot be maintained. This was also Russell's opinion in the *Principles of Mathematics*. "M. Couturat, in his admirable work on Leibniz, states roundly that Symbolic Logic can only be built up from the standpoint of extension," Russell says (p. 66), and adds, "But as a matter of fact, there are positions intermediate between pure intension and pure extension, and it is in these intermediate regions that Symbolic Logic has its lair." This does not, however, mean that Russell would at that time have adhered to interpretation (12)—on the contrary he found it "highly doubtful" whether (12) and (1) were the "same proposition" (p. 36). In what way he regarded the "lair" of symbolic logic intermediate between pure extension and pure intension is not quite clear, but in fact he seems to have adopted an interpretation of (1), which is indeed intermediate between the pure extensional and the pure intensional view, but is so in a much more trivial way than formulation (12).

Actually, a purely extensional interpretation of (1) lapses into a tautology because we interpret both "man" and "mortal" extensionally. In (12) we have interpreted both "man" and "mortal" intensionally, leaving what is extensional about (1) to the reference of the variable. However, there is also a third possibility, that of interpreting "man," or more strictly speaking "all men" extensionally, while interpreting the predicate "mortal" intensionally.

We may arrive at this interpretation of (1) in the following way. Many logicians have conceived of the statement

(13)   Socrates is mortal

as a special instance of a statement of the form

(14)   All S are P,   1887818

namely the instance in which there is just one S. Now there are three ways of doing this. One is the purely intensional way. We replace Socrates with a property S_0, which comprises all Socrates' properties, and take (13) as stating that mortality is one of these properties. We write, that is, (13) in the form

(15) $S_0 = XM$,

which is of the same form as (2). This might be called the Leibnizian way of reducing (13) to a universal affirmative.

The second way is this. We introduce a predicate called "x socratizes," which we write "$S_0(x)$," and interpret (13) in the form

(16) $(x)(S_0(x) \supset M(x))$.

This might be called the Quinean way of reducing (13) to a universal affirmative.[5]

There is, however, a third way of conceiving (13) as a special instance of (14), which reduces a universal affirmative to a statement of the form (13) rather than the other way round. This is the idea of treating (1) as if it were a subject-predicate sentence, with the difference, that the subject here is in the plural, whereas in (13) it is in the singular. If conceived of in this way (1) could (adopting the notation of (8)(a)) be written in the form

(17) $M(a_1)$ & $M(a_2)$ & . . . & $M(a_m)$.

Formula (17) is certainly not logically equivalent to (12), but it is not logically equivalent to (10) either, and thus it is no tautology. (13) is the special instance of (17) in which the conjunction contains just one member.

6. Now there is strong evidence for the view that this was the rendering of (1) which Russell in *Principles of Mathematics* adhered to.[6] Against

5. See Quine, ML, sec. 37. I have criticized this analysis of singular terms in BOT, section VIII: 3.
6. See sections 59–61. To be sure, Russell's account here is rather complicated. On the one hand, he tends to make a distinction between "every" and "all," thinking that the former gives rise to a "propositional" conjunction, the latter to a "numerical" conjunction. This would suggest that according to Russell's view here (17) is a rendering of "Every man is mortal" rather than "All men are mortal," but, on the other hand, Russell admits (p. 57) that "all" sometimes gives rise to a "propositional conjunction." I should interpret Russell as thinking that the distinction between "numerical" and "propositional" conjunction does not matter in respect of sentences of this type.

it one may raise the objection that, though (17) is equivalent to (1), it cannot state the same thing as (1), since it does not state that $a_1, a_2, \ldots,$ a_m are men and certainly not that they are all men. (17) states of all individuals which actually are men that they are mortal, but it does not state that all men are mortal.

This may seem so obvious that it makes (17) sound naive as a rendering of (1). But the matter cannot be settled as simply as that. Compare the sentence

(18)   All John's sons are tall

with the singular sentence

(19)   John's son is tall,

which will be used if John has only one son. Sentence (19) is often (but not always) used as what I call a semantic subject-predicate statement the semantic subject of which is John's son. This means that it is used to *characterize* a certain person as tall in contradistinction to other persons who are not tall. As I have argued elsewhere (BOT, section VIII:4), when (19) is used in this way, the function of the phrase "John's son" is purely *referential*. Its function is to *indicate* or *identify*[7] the object of which we are speaking, not to characterize a given object as John's son. (We cannot characterize an object unless we have indicated what object we are speaking of.) This again means that the intension of the expression "John's son" does not enter into the semantics of (19) in this interpretation; (19) is on this interpretation logically equivalent to

(20)   Jim is tall,

if "Jim" is the name of John's son. As soon as we take (19) to state something different from (20), we interpret it in a different way. For instance it may be interpreted as a statement about *John,* characterizing him as a person whose only son is tall, in contradistinction to persons who do not possess this property; and then the intension of the expression "John's son" is of course not irrelevant for the semantics of (19).

Now the same applies to plural reference. Suppose that John has three sons, Jim, Charles and Fred. Then the statement

(21)   Jim, Charles and Fred are tall

can be regarded as a semantic subject-predicate statement with a plural semantic subject, which states the same thing as

(22)   Jim is tall and Charles is tall and Fred is tall.

---

7. The use of the word "identify" in this context I take from ES, p. 629. Black's discussion has also inspired some other formulations in this paper.

Now the sentence

(23)   The sons of John are tall

is often interpreted as a subject-predicate sentence with a plural subject, and then it is taken to state what (21) and (22) state.

Let us now return to sentence (18). Is it not sometimes interpreted in exactly the way we have interpreted (23)? Is not the phrase "All John's sons" sometimes used purely referentially to indicate what persons we are speaking of? And isn't the same true of other sentences of the form (14)?

I think the answer to these questions is yes. To be sure, it is not a very "natural" interpretation. But even unnatural interpretations sometimes are correct. The unnaturalness of this interpretation will be manifest if we consider the sentence

(24)   All men are men.

This statement has been considered a paradigm case of a tautological statement, but if we take "tautology" in the Wittgensteinian sense this is so only if it is interpreted in the same way as (1) in (12), that is as

(25) $(x)(H(x) \supset H(x))$.

If we interpret it as (1) in (17), we get

(26) $H(a_1)$ & $H(a_2)$ & . . . & $H(a_m)$,

which is not tautological.[8]

The fact that the interpretation (17) of (1) is more unnatural than interpretation (12) does not, however, make it entirely wrong. Actually ordinary language is slightly ambiguous here. It is ambiguous in this respect, as it is ambiguous in respect of sentence (19). The fact that (19) is ambiguous does not matter in most uses of such sentences. But as I have shown elsewhere (BOT, section VIII: 5) the ambiguity accounts for the paradox of identity in modal contexts. Something similar is true of sentence (1). In some contexts it is clear what interpretation is meant, and then we need not bother about a possible ambiguity on principle. In some other cases it is irrelevant what is meant, and then the ambiguity does not matter. But in certain cases we have a tendency to interpret (1) in two different ways and to switch over from the one interpretation to the other without noticing it. And it is then that a fairly unambiguous symbolic notation is of great help. That is one of the greatest advantages of symbolic logic.

8. The same is of course true of "John's son is a son of John's," conceived of as a semantic subject-predicate statement the semantic subject of which is "John's son." This statement is, to be sure uninformative, and thus "tautological" in a sense, but not in the Wittgensteinian sense of having a vacuous content.

7. The introduction of interpretation (12) of (1) meant a great progress in philosophical analysis. The superiority of this notation can be illustrated by the fact that the other interpretations can be formalized within its framework. Thus interpretation (2) can be given the form

(27) $L[(x)(H(x) \supset M(x))]$.

where the operator "L" stands for "logically true" (in one interpretation of this notion). This shows that it is misleading to a certain extent to say that the intensional interpretation is "analytic." For if "analytic" means the same as "tautological" what is taugological on this interpretation is statement (12), not the metastatement (27)—this can be characterized as a nontautological (singular) statement about the concepts "man" and "mortal."

The purely extensional interpretation (10) can be given the form

(28) $(x)(x = a_1 \lor x = a_2 \lor \ldots \lor x = a_m$
$\supset x = b_1 \lor x = b_2 \lor \ldots \lor x = b_n)$

Finally the mixed interpretation (17) can be given the form

(29) $(x)(x = a_1 \lor x = a_2 \lor \ldots \lor x = a_m \supset M(x))$.

In this formulation we clearly see the difference between the different interpretations.

Despite its merit, interpretation (12) of (1) is not entirely unproblematic. The problem concerns the universe of discourse to which the quantifier variable in (12) refers. This should be in some way indicated, but in what way? Here the logicians seem to lapse in some sort of mystification.

Frege said that a universal statement states a relationship between two concepts (FA, p. 60). If we were to take him literally this would mean that in fact he takes an intensional view of (1).[9] The error here is that he leaves out the unavoidable reference to the universe of discourse in (12). If we characterize (12) as stating a relationship between certain entities, the extensional feature of (12) means that it does not state a relationship just between the two concepts "man" and "mortal," but between these two concepts *and the universe of discourse.* Without reference to the universe of discourse the quantifier loses its sense, and this is also true of the variable *"x."*

But how is the universe of discourse given? It cannot be given as the class of objects which form the extension of a certain property, for a property determines an extension only relatively to a universe of dis-

9. I do not think he should be taken literally. In the terminology of Kauppi (LL, p. 8) one could perhaps interpret him as thinking that a universal statement expresses an "extensional" relationship between two concepts. But if we consider what kind of relationship that may be, we arrive at the analysis given in the text.

course given in advance. Moreover, if the universe of discourse is specified as the extension of a property, say, U, then the introduction of the property U would suggest that (12) ought to be replaced by the formula

(30) $(x)(U(x) \supset (H(x) \supset M(x)))$,

which would lead to an infinite regress.

Frege does not pay much attention to the universe of discourse. In the *Begriffsschrift* he just says that the quantifier indicates that the function to which it refers "is a fact whatever we take its argument to be" (TPW, p. 16). This was formulated in the idyllic time when one still thought that this phrase had a definite sense. It obviously has not. In the paper "On Denoting," in which Russell enthusiastically switched from his earlier conception of the semantics of "all" to the new conception in accordance with (12), he expresses himself as vaguely as Frege; he just states that "C (everything) means 'C(x) is always true' " (LK, p. 42). In *Principia Mathematica*, however, he is more explicit about the matter. Speaking of formalization (12) he states (p. 45f.): "The advantage of this form is that the values which the variable may take are given by the function to which it is the argument: the values which the variable may take are all those with which the function is significant." This means that the values which the variable *"x"* in (12) may take are determined by the propositional function *"H(x) $\supset$ M(x),"* they are those values for which this propositional function is significant. But this means also that he tends to make (12) intensional after all, the universe of discourse being in a way logically inherent in the properties to which (1) refers. Even a range of significance taken in extension can only be determined in relation to a given universe of discourse.

Wittgenstein tries to overcome the difficulty by the formulation "If the objects are given, then at the same time we are given *all* objects" (*Tractatus* 5.524). This may be interpreted as follows: the fact that all men are given as objects does not imply the fact that these objects are given as constituting *all* men. But if all the objects of our universe of discourse are given, then the fact that they constitute *all* objects is also given (cf. Stenius, WT, p. 153). This may be taken as one way of expressing the fact that the universe of discourse must be given extensionally and not intensionally by some characterizing property. But it does not solve the problem of how the universe of discourse can be given extensionally.

To be sure, if the universe of discourse is finite and limited we can think of it as given by an enumeration of the objects it contains. But how is it to be given if the universe is infinite or of an unfeasible size?

I have not been able to solve this problem in a satisfactory way. This means that I have, after all, a feeling of uneasiness about (12) as a formalization of (1). Should really the statement "All men are mortal" be about an indeterminate and perhaps indeterminable universe of discourse? In this respect formalization (17) is more satisfactory.

I think the relative clarity of formalization (12) is founded on the relative clarity of the *image* we form of the universe of discourse. In the *Principles of Mathematics* Russell says at one place (p. 66): "It is essential that the classes with which we are concerned should be composed of terms, and should not be predicates or concepts, for a class must be definite when its terms are given. . . . On the other hand, if we take extensions pure, our class is defined by enumeration of its terms, and this method will not allow us to deal, as Symbolic Logic does, with infinite classes." But at another place (p. 69) he states that the impossibility of defining infinite classes extensionally is "purely psychological": "logically, the extensional definition appears to be equally applicable to infinite classes, but practically, if we were to attempt it, Death would cut short our laudable endeavour before it had attained its goal." If we strip from this its lofty logical realism and apply it to the universe of discourse, I think it means that we allow ourselves to operate with an image of the universe of discourse as being given by enumeration even though we know that such an enumeration cannot be performed. The only alternative is the adoption of a strongly finitistic attitude to mathematics, which has its own disadvantages. Actually I think we can adopt this image without much confusion, if only we are aware of the fact that we form it and of the fact that what we then form is just a kind of fictive image and not the representation of a logical reality.

References

Black, Max. "The Elusiveness of Sets," *The Review of Metaphysics*, 24 (1972) 614–636. (ES)

Couturat, Louis. *La Logique de Leibniz*. Hildesheim, 1961. (LL).

Frege, G. *The Foundations of Arithmetic*. Trans. J. L. Austin. Oxford, 1953. (FA).

_____. *Translations from the Philosophical Writings of Gottlob Frege*. Ed. P. Geach and M. Black. Oxford (TPW).

Kauppi, Raili. *Einführung in die Theorie der Begriffssysteme*. (Acta Universitatis Tamperensis, ser. A, vol. 15). Helsinki, 1967. (ETB).

_____. *Über die Leibnizsche Logik*. (Acta Philosophica Fennica XII). Helsinki, 1960. (LL).

Leibniz, Gottfried Wilhelm. *Fragmente zur Logik*. Ausgewählt, übersetzt und erläutert von Franz Schmidt. Berlin, 1960. (FL).

_____. *Opuscules et Fragments inédits de Leibniz, extraits par Louis Couturat*. Hildsheim, 1961. (OFI).

_____. *Logical Paper*. Trans. and ed. G. H. R. Parkinson. Oxford, 1966. (LP).

Quine, Willard Van Orman. *Methods of Logic*. London, 1958. 2nd edition. (ML).

Russell, Bertrand. *The Principles of Mathematics*. 2nd edition. London, 1937. (PoM).

_____. *Logic and Knowledge*. London, 1956. (LK).

Stenius, Erik. *Wittgenstein's Tractatus*. Oxford, 1960. (WT).

_____. "Beginning with Ordinary Things," *Synthese*, 19 (1968–69). Reprinted in *Words and Objections, Essays on the Work of W. V. Quine.* Ed. Donald Davidson and Jaakko Hintikka. Dordrecht, 1969. (BOT).

Whitehead, Alfred North, and Russell, Bertrand. *Principia Mathematica.* Cambridge, 1927. (PM).

Wittgenstein, Ludwig. *Tractatus Logico-Philosophicus.* Trans. D. F. Pears and B. F. Mc-Guiness. London, 1961.

Notes on the Form of Certain Elementary Facts

N. L. Wilson

McMaster University

I

(1) Jones buttered the toast in the bathroom at midnight.

That toast[1] bids fair to join Descartes' piece of wax, the morning star and the author of Waverley as a classic example. Now one of the legacies of mathematical logic and its immense prestige is the notion that an atomic sentence is of the same form as, say, 'P(3)' or 'G(3,2)' – 'Three is prime', 'Three is greater than two'. Thus we will have 'Chicago is large' and 'Phaedo is taller than Simmias' as being "typical" atomic sentences of English, corresponding to typical facts. We have all known this to be wrong but it is only recently that people have come to realize how seriously wrong it is. Attention has mostly been directed to action sentences, but in this paper we shall be more concerned with one aspect of the more general problem of adverbial modifiers.

Consider (1) above and (2):

(2) Jones buttered the toast.

Donald Davidson's problem is to analyze (1) in such a way that it is clear how (1) can entail (2), which apparently it does. I shall argue on the contrary that both (1) and (2) are ill-formed as they stand; neither entails anything. Hence this particular problem evaporates – leaving, of course many other problems behind.

Some introductory remarks. I shall regard a fact as a true proposition. After all, it seems to be a matter of indifference whether we say: It is a fact that Socrates took hemlock, or, It is a true proposition that Socrates

---

1. See Donald Davidson, "The Logical Form of Action Sentences," in Nicholas Rescher, ed., *The Logic of Decision and Action* (University of Pittsburgh Press, 1966), pp. 81–95. The original example (p. 82) is, 'Jones buttered the toast slowly, deliberately, in the bathroom, with a knife at midnight'. This was presumably inspired by Kenny's more sanguinary example, 'Brutus killed Caesar in Pompey's theatre with a knife out of jealousy clumsily on the Ides of March'. See A. C. Kenny, *Action, Emotion and Will* (London: Routledge and Kegan Paul, 1963), p 160.

took hemlock. To this view there is the standard rhetorical objection: What do you do with false propositions? The answer is that you don't have to do anything with them, except perhaps to call them nonfacts. They are *there,* of course, but they do not in any way constitute the world construed as the totality of facts.

Charles Baylis and I discussed the question of facts on several occasions. He wants to say that a fact is not a true proposition but rather that which makes a true proposition true. It took me a long time to realize that if we take propositions to be *meanings,* that is, intensional entities, whose identity conditions are given in terms of logical or analytic equivalence, then Baylis is unquestionably right. A fact cannot be a true proposition. The concrete man, Socrates, is a constituent of the fact that Socrates took hemlock, but, not being a "meaning" he cannot be a constituent of the intensional proposition that Socrates took hemlock. It seems to me that *if* one is going to hold that a fact is a true proposition, then he must abandon semantics based on "meaning" and opt for something like the semantics of significance (G-designation) I proposed for general semantics.[2] We say that 'Socrates' signifies the individual, Socrates, 'pale' signifies the property, paleness, 'Socrates is pale' signifies the proposition (G-proposition, that is, not intensional proposition) that Socrates is pale. A consequence of this shift, it seems to me, is that we must renounce all but atomic facts. There is nothing in the world corresponding to 'and', 'or', 'not', 'some', 'all', or 'identical with'. In *this* sense logic has nothing to do with metaphysics. The argument, very sketchily, is this: Suppose we grant the existence of molecular and general propositions, including facts. Then we must admit the multiply general fact that some individual drank hemlock and is identical with all and only teachers of Plato. This is presumably identical with the fact that the teacher of Plato drank hemlock, which (since the teacher of Plato is identical with Socrates) is in turn identical with the *atomic* fact that Socrates drank hemlock. Similarly, if it is a fact that Socrates is red then (since red is identical with the color of boiled lobster) that fact is identical with the fact that Socrates is the color of boiled lobster. We conclude that there are no multiply general facts of the sort in question, and, more generally, that there are no logically complex facts. If I speak of the fact that Socrates drank (some) hemlock, or the fact that Philip is drunk at some time, then that alleged fact is only a fact honoris causa, as it were.

One wishes it were possible to be clearer about facts. The main difficulty I see has to do with the indeterminacy of facts. Now the world itself is fully specific or determinate. (Forget quantum theory and statistical

2. See N. L. Wilson, *The Concept of Language* (University of Toronto Press), 1959. By "general semantics" I mean the field which seeks *general* definitions of 'G-designates', 'logically true', 'true' and, of course, 'language'.

mechanics.) That is to say, for every yes or no question, couched in as specific terms as you please, there is a true yes or no answer. Therefore, if—and I tend to follow *Tractatus* (1.1) here—the world is the totality of facts, then every fact is fully determinate. (Every fact? Well, you've got to have *some* determinate facts. Indeterminate facts riding piggy-back on the determinate ones would seem to be excess baggage.) But on the other hand all the facts that we will be concerned with are indeterminate to a degree. Suppose it is a fact that Socrates is pale. How pale? Chalk pale? Ashen pale? The point is that there can be a certain amount of variation in the fact but any variant would still make our sentence true. Further-more, the indeterminacy seems to be essential for the utility of a language: the more determinate a statement, the more difficult it is to know whether it is true or false.

It is sometimes thought that this indeterminacy (and, what is not quite the same, vagueness) is peculiar to our familiar properties, whereas in-dividuals are quite clear and straightforward. This illusion perhaps lies at the bottom of what would be called temperamental nominalism. ("I just can't believe in properties!") I call it an illusion because the alleged clarity of individuals rests on the purely accidental fact that familiar in-dividuals are for the most part solid objects surrounded on five sides by air. But the Atlantic and Pacific Oceans are individuals and yet there is no sharp boundary between them—unless one wants to pretend that there is one grain of sand that is the southernmost tip of South America. And even in the case of a human being there is vagueness. Does a person's hair count as part of him? The contents of his alimentary canal? His clothing? An officer is not supposed to touch an enlisted man. (If he does, the latter is entitled to haul off and sock him.) One can imagine an officer, taxed with the action, replying, "I didn't touch *him,* I touched his tunic." And even if "touching him" were precise (not vague) it is nonspecific as between touching him on the shoulder, the elbow and so on. My point— tangential, to be sure—is that whatever there is about properties that makes us uncomfortable about recognizing them can be matched by some-thing just about as messy in connection with individuals.

But I think we are forced to concede that there is an element of make-believe about our ontology of facts. Our facts just aren't there, since our facts are "abstract" or indeterminate (as *red* is abstract relative to any specific shade of red), and nothing real is abstract. There is a real ontology of *fully specific* facts and there is no such fact that could not be reported by some statement which exactly captures it (nothing ineffable), but by the same token no such fact can be *exactly* captured by the somewhat nonspecific linguistic resources *we ordinarily use*. I *don't* want to say that our atomic sentences capture shadowy things that approximate to facts. I would rather say that they approximately capture facts. The point of pretending to believe in our make-believe facts is that some of the things we shall be led to say about them are things that, obviously, we will be able to say about real facts. This is, I daresay, metaphysics. I follow Aristotle in holding that we can discover something about the general structure of reality by examining the structure of what we say about the world. That we can make such discoveries is due to the fact that we talk the way we do just because the world is the way it is.

There is a tone of dogmatism in the last few paragraphs. I am optimistically assuming that the reader will share my intuitions, or at least entertain them for the moment. If he does not, and can offer reasons why I don't have to concede that there is something fishy about "our facts" then I should be very happy. It does not matter in any case, because what I have offered rather dogmatically is not something that what I have to say will depend on. It now remains to say what I have to say. (That (1) and (2) above are ill-formed.)

II

In his review[3] of Julius Weinberg's *Nicholaus of Autrecourt* Peter Geach writes (p. 244), "Such expressions as 'at time *t*' . . . are out of place in expounding scholastic views of time and motion. For a scholastic, 'Socrates is sitting' is a complete proposition, *enuntiabile,* which is sometimes true, sometimes false; not an incomplete expression requiring a further phrase like 'at time *t*' to make it into an assertion." There are perhaps some moderns who are prepared to take the same line. Now we can take

(3)   Socrates is sitting

as a complete sentence if we read the verb as tensed:

(3')   Socrates is-now sitting [which is false].

Or if we read the verb as untensed and suppose that there is a tacit egocentric temporal adverb which, when supplied, gives us

(3″)   Socrates is now sitting.

And I suppose we can even make sense of it if we are prepared to talk of truth at such and such a time. But apart from these alternatives it seems as if we must take (3) as either ill-formed (like 'Phaedo is taller than') if taken at face value, or else as elliptical for

3. *Mind,* 58 (1949), 238–245. The passage from this is quoted by A. N. Prior, in *Past Present and Future* (Oxford, 1967), p. 15 and the citation is mentioned in R. L. Clark, "Concerning the Logic of Predicate Modifiers," *Nous,* 4 (1970), 322.

(4) Socrates is sitting at some time [which is true].

The reason is that (3), with an untensed verb, doesn't seem to have a truth value. (Well, *what* truth value?) And further,

(5) Socrates is sitting and it is not the case that Socrates is sitting at some time

seems to be absurd. And my suggestion is that the absurdity can be looked upon as stemming from the ill-formedness of the first conjunct or looked upon as stemming from the fact that the first conjunct is elliptical for what the second conjunct denies.

I don't want to cross swords with tense-logicians so I shall make it clear that it's case of: *If* we take 'is' as untensed, and *if* we take truth in the Tarskian sense according to which a sentence is true or false *simpliciter* and 'true' cannot take temporal adverbs, *then* we must disqualify (3) as a sentence and replace it by (4). The motive for ignoring other possibilities is that we hope to find out something about the form of facts by looking at complete, nonelliptical, nonegocentric (i.e., non-token-reflexive), unambiguous sentences in primitive notation, which allegedly report facts.

Of course even (4) does not report a fact, not even a make-believe fact, since it contains the quantifier 'some'. But perhaps the following do:

(6) Socrates is sitting at noon on August 31.
(7) Philip is drunk at noon on August 31, 350 B.C.

The "facts" these sentences report, supposing them to be true, are make-believe facts, to be sure, but from here on in I shall drop the qualification "make-believe." What seems clear is that some elementary facts, *real* facts, that is, are comprised of an individual, a monadic property, and a time and cannot be comprised of fewer components. Categorizing sentences, like 'Socrates is human' and 'Kant is a philosopher' are a bit tricky and I do not propose dealing with them.

Now it might be thought that exactly the same line of argument that showed that (3) must be read as (4) could be adduced to show that (7) is either incomplete, or elliptical for

(8) Philip is drunk at noon on August 31, 350 B.C. at some place.

Certainly one might reasonably wish to know whether Philip was drunk in the decent seclusion of his palace or was staggering about in public. Nevertheless I believe this line must be resisted. Let us write 'p' for 'Philip', 'D' for 'drunk', 't_1' for 'noon on August 31, 350 B.C.' and 'P' as a variable ranging over places, and consider, in analogy to (5),

(9) p is D at t_1 & $-(\exists P)$ (p is D at t_1 at P).

This is not logically false and is not obviously self-contradictory. But it is "absurd." And it is at least open to us to take the second conjunct as ill-formed or "over-inflated." We regiment (8) to 'There is some place such that Philip is drunk at noon on August 31, 350 B.C., and Philip is at that place on August 31, 350 B.C.'[4], i.e.,

(8') $(\exists P)$ (p is D at t_1 & p is at P at t_1).

Now (9) becomes

(9') p is D at t_1 & $-(\exists P)$ (p is D at t_1 & p is at P at t_1)

which is logically equivalent to

(10) p is D at t_1 & $-(\exists P)$ (p is at P at t_1).

But even (10) is neither logically false nor obviously self-contradictory. It is, however, incompatible with the axioms of individuation I laid down for individuals in "Space, Time and Individuals."[5] Specifically it is inconsistent with the necessary nonlogical principle that if an individual has a nonspatial property at a time, it has a place at that time:

(11) x is Q at $t \supset (\exists P)$ (x is at P at t).

This principle is necessary relative to what I take to be the principles of individuation implicit in an ordinary language. At any rate, this principle, along with 'p is D at t_1' does imply our (8') and, by doing so, does refute (10).

There are two difficulties, one concerning the petitio involved in invoking (11) and the other involving apparent counter-examples to (11). The latter first. For example,

(12) Beethoven is revered in 1970.

It does not follow that Beethoven has a place in 1970. But like all the counter-examples, the sentence doesn't say quite what it appears to be saying. It really says that people revere Beethoven in 1970. So we prohibit passive voice sentences from going in as antecedent of (11). But even some actives are suspect:

4. This is reminiscent of a maneuver adopted by Davidson, op. cit.

5. *Journal of Philosophy*, 52 (1955), 589–598. The axioms are: (B1) Every individual occupies some place at some time. (B2) Every individual occupies at most one place at a time. (B3) Two individuals occupying the same place at the same time are identical. (B4) If an individual occupies a place at a time, it has some nonspatial property at that time, and (B5)—what I am invoking here—if an individual has a nonspatial property at a time it occupies a place at that time. And then the complicated (B6), which is roughly: The individual at *this* place at *this* time is identical with the individual at *that* place at *that* time, if and only if there is a fulled, non-doubling-back world line going from the first place-time to the second place-time. From these axioms there follow some theorems, one of which makes it reasonably clear what we *mean* in saying that the man who wrote Marmion in 1807 is identical with the man who wrote Waverley in 1814.

(13)   Beethoven delights audiences in 1970.

But here again, it is not Beethoven, but performances of his music, that delights audiences in 1970. And similarly for

(14)   He blew up the aircraft in the air over Austria [but he was safely on the ground in Switzerland at the time].

This is an (apparent) counter-example, not so much to (11) actually, as to the rule that a sentence of the form '*x* is *Q* (or did *A*) at *P*' is to be regimented to '*x* was at *P* at a time he was *Q* (or did *A*)'. This is the "remote control problem."[6] We first rewrite (14) as 'He did things which eventually caused the aircraft to blow up in the air over Austria' [and at the time he did them he was where he did them, namely, in Switzerland] and then regiment.

I shall take it that all apparent counter-examples can be handled by non-ad hoc means. I say "non-ad hoc" because they can be recast in a more explicit form or in a more elementary form (as the active voice is more elementary than the passive) which does not represent a counter-example to (11) or anything else we want.

Now the question of petitio. Our problem is to explain the intuitively felt absurdity of (9) and to avoid it. There is the suggestion that it is in the same case as (5), that it is to be accounted for by treating the first conjunct as elliptical for what the second conjunct denies and that when the ellipsis is filled in we have a straightforward logical contradiction. I propose to take the more elaborate course: to regard the second conjunct as ill-formed, to regiment it as (8′) so that (9) becomes equivalent to (10), which in turn is refuted by appeal to the general principle, (11). That this begs the question is shown by the fact that the other side will not allow appeal to (11) because they regard the antecedent as either ill-formed (taken at face value) or as elliptical for '(∃*P*) (*x* is *Q* at *t* at *P*)'. I wish there were some decisive argument against the other side but I am afraid there is not. What does seem clear is that we can have either (8) or (8′), but not both—at least not without a fair amount of finagling. Of course, one can introduce (8) and *define* it to mean (8′), but that is irrelevant to the present aim, which is to say something about the structure of facts by getting into the position of saying: *these* linguistic resources are necessary to report the facts that are there to be reported, *those* resources are redundant. Moreover, one actually can have both (8) and (8′) as primitive forms, if he wants, provided he is willing to requisition a big, ugly bicon-

6. It comes up in connection with Davidson's example in E. J. Lemmon's suggestion that although Jones buttered the toast in the bathroom he himself was outside the bathroom door and did the deed with a long-handled knife. We may conclude that it is sometimes not clear whether a place-expression is intended to locate the agent or the patient.

ditional axiom connecting them. But again, this maneuver is uninteresting because it gives up the quest for minimal resources.

However, there are perhaps a number of nondecisive considerations which, collectively, carry quite a bit of weight. I am holding that (8) is ill-formed as it stands. Correlatively, I am holding that

(15)   Philip is drunk at noon on August 31, 350 B.C. in the palace

is ill-formed and could not report a fact of the same form. Facts just don't have that kind of structure. (15) is to be regimented to:

(15′)   Philip is drunk at noon on August 31, 350 B.C. and Philip is in the palace at noon on August 31, 350 B.C.

and this does not report a fact because (in my view) there are no conjunctive facts. (But that's a different story which needn't be told here.) When we ask 'Where was Philip drunk?' our question has to be regimented to 'Where was Philip when (at the time(s)) he was drunk?' It might be suggested[7] that the procedure here gives to time a certain preferred status. Why not turn things around and say that 'When?' questions have to be regimented, so that 'When was Philip drunk?' becomes 'When was Philip at the place(s) he was drunk at?' Now it might be that Philip is drunk and in the agora on Wednesday and is sober all the rest of the week and is in the agora on Tuesday and Thursday, in which case our original question is answered by 'Wednesday' and the suggested regimentation is answered by 'Tuesday, Wednesday and Thursday'. Thus this kind of regimentation won't work. So if we grant a certain preferred status to time it's because time actually has it. The point is that Philip can be at the same place at different times but he cannot be at different places at the same time. Time is just not on all fours with space. Again, things have qualities at times—different qualities at different times—and things have places at times—different places at different times. So it looks as though places and nonspatial qualities belong together, with times left outside. If we are willing to accept 'x is at P at t' as being well-formed, we have no reason to cavil at 'x is Q at t' even though we shall insist that if x is at P at t then x has a nonspatial quality at t, and that if x is Q at t, then x has a place at t.

Now a great deal of this informal disquisition would have to be disallowed by the other side. But ceteris paribus we would have no reason to want to disallow it. This constitutes what seems to me to be reasonably weighty circumstantial evidence on behalf of my own proposal—or, more accurately, evidence for the wisdom of adopting my proposal.

The point comes out from another direction. The sentence 'Philip is

7. And was suggested to me by R. L. Clark.

drunk at noon on Wednesday' carries the suggestion, as a sort of pseudo-corollary, that perhaps Philip was not drunk at noon on Thursday. At any rate the conjunction, 'Philip is drunk at noon on Wednesday but maybe he is sober at noon on Thursday' runs trippingly off the tongue. But 'Philip is drunk at noon on Wednesday in the palace but maybe he is sober at noon on Wednesday in the agora' does not run trippingly off the tongue at all. It is absurd. And this fact has the force of tending to cancel out any inclination we might have to regard (9) and (5) as parallel and to handle the absurdity of the one in a fashion similar to that for handling the absurdity of the other.

A final observation.

(16)   There was a mole on his shoulder (at some time).
(17)   There was a sandcastle on his (private) beach (at some time).

These are of the same form and 'on' is being used in the same senses in both. But consider

(18)   Philip was sunburned on his shoulder (at some time).
(19)   Philip was sunburned on his beach (at some time).

These appear to be different in form, or at least somehow different. Perhaps linguisticians could show that they have different deep structures, but offhand I doubt it. We are able to account for the difference because we regiment (19) to: 'There is a time such that Philip was sunburned (or, got a sunburn, if you prefer) at that time and was on his beach at that time'. We can leave (18) alone or perhaps recast it as 'Philip's shoulder is sunburned at some time'. The point is, we can distinguish two kinds of *where* questions: those like 'Where was he [when he was] drunk?', which ask for the location of the individual, and those like 'Where was he itchy?', which do not ask for the location of the individual but do ask for the location of the itch on that individual. I doubt that the other side can make sense of the distinction.

Now to return to Davidson's (1) and (2). What seems to me beyond question is that at least one of them is ill-formed. I have argued — not quite decisively — that both are ill-formed. In either case the problem of explaining the alleged entailment of (2) by (1) vanishes. And there were a few by no means inconsequential incidental results. Atomic sentences (and their corresponding make-believe facts and their corresponding "real" facts) have a certain "right" form. They must contain neither too little nor too much. In the family of cases in question, that means there must be a time-expression and there must *not* be both a place-expression and an ordinary property expression. Moreover the syntax of time expressions and the syntax of place expressions are manifestly quite different.

The Ultimate Justification
of Moral Rules

Robert Binkley

University of Western Ontario

To justify a thing is to show it to be reasonable, that is, to exhibit it as the outcome of a legitimate reasoning process. In the present paper I inquire how this might be done in the case of moral rules, and in particular, how it might be done in a way that does not presuppose prior acceptance of any moral rules. (That is what makes the justifications I consider *ultimate*.) I shall suggest certain very general conditions that must be met by any such justification if it is to satisfactorily justify the rule *as moral*. Finally, I shall suggest, in a highly schematic way, a possible form that such justifications might take.

There are two different ways in which a moral rule can be exhibited as the outcome of a piece of reasoning, and there are correspondingly two different kinds of justification. I shall distinguish them by Herbert Feigl's terms, *validation* and *vindication*,[1] though attaching perhaps somewhat different meanings to them.

The distinction is one of logical form, and is most clearly seen if we imagine the reasoning to be expressed formally as a deduction with its conclusion as the last line. Then in the *validation* of a moral rule the last line is a formulation of the moral rule itself. In the case of *vindication*, the last line is a formulation of the decision to accept the moral rule. (I use "decision" here, but for present purposes it is unnecessary to distinguish it from other words in the area such as "choice," "volition," "intention," "willing," etc.) Validation is first-level reasoning concerning the content of what is to be accepted. Vindication is second-level reasoning concerning the practical decision to become a certain sort of person, namely one who accepts a certain content.

If a justification of either kind is to be acceptable, then the reasoning that constitutes it must satisfy two conditions. In the first place, the reasoning must be valid; that is, it must obey the relevant principles of rea-

1. Herbert Feigl, "Validation and Vindication: An Analysis of the Nature and the Limits of Ethical Arguments," in Sellars and Hospers, eds., *Readings in Ethical Theory* (New York, 1952), pp. 667–680.

soning. (In the case of vindication, principles of practical reasoning.[2]) For the second condition, we must distinguish between justifications that are acceptable absolutely and those that are acceptable relative to an agent. In the second case, it is required that all the premises of the reasoning be in fact accepted by the agent. In the first it is required that they be true, or more generally, that they be objectively acceptable. (The meaning of this last phrase will be gone into later on; for the moment it may perhaps coast along on the slogan "holding for all rational beings.")

The first point for which I wish to argue is that there can be no such thing as an acceptable ultimate validation of a moral rule, so that if any moral rule is to be ultimately justified at all, it must be by an ultimate vindication.

The argument is the familiar and tedious one of the gap between "is" and "ought." Such a validation would require an "ought" in the conclusion, but if it is to be ultimate, there can be no "ought" in the premises; principles of reasoning never give you something for nothing, and so such reasoning could not be valid.

It might be objected that I am here taking an overly narrow and deductive view of logic; perhaps a more generous notion of what principles of reasoning can authorize would remove the difficulty. For example, there is supposed to be such a thing as *inductive* logic. Perhaps it could do the job. Unfortunately, inductive logic hardly seems applicable. It is designed to lead us from a prior knowledge of particular cases to a knowledge of generalities. Moral rules, however, are supposed to dictate to particular cases, not to be derived from them, and knowledge of the rules must come first.

But then perhaps what is required is a logic of confirmation. We bring the moral rule to the particular case and then regard it as justified, or at least confirmed to some extent, if the particular case does not refute it. The trouble with this is that it is not clear how a particular case could refute or fail to refute, a moral rule. The problem is not simply, as it is in science, that when the particular case contradicts the rule the blame may be shifted to some other rule, or to "experimental error." The problem is to see how the particular case can contradict the rule in the first place.

Let the rule in question be that one ought to do an action of kind A when in circumstances of kind C, and suppose that I come to a particular case of C. My rule then tells me that I ought to perform an action of kind A. How can the particular case contradict that, since the only way I have of finding out what I ought to do in a particular case is to apply my moral

2. I have tried to define a sense of "valid" applicable both to theoretical and to practical reasoning in "A Theory of Practical Reason," *The Philosophical Review*, 74 (1965), 423–448. The general approach of that paper lies behind many of the points made here, but the details are not presupposed.

rules to it? Suppose I choose not to do A. Then I have broken the rule, but that is not a contradiction of it. Perhaps I not only choose not to do A but do so as a decision of principle, as Hare has suggested. That is, I reject the rule in favor of some other, say, that one ought to do A' in C. Here again, nothing in the particular case has contradicted the rule. Or, to put it another way, the only thing in the particular case that has contradicted the rule is me. That a person changes his mind about a rule is no proof that it is mistaken.

Perhaps instead of the logic of confirmation we need a special moral logic to carry us from the premises to the conclusion of our ultimate validation. But it is hard to know what such a logic could be like. Perhaps it will contain principles of inference to the effect that from such and such factual premises one may infer such and such a deontic conclusion. But such a principle of inference would seem to be nothing but a moral rule in disguise, and so the validation, whatever its merits, would not count as an ultimate one.

I suspect that the conclusion that moral rules cannot ultimately be validated will not come as a surprise to many of my readers; received opinion in fact seems to be that morality is not ultimately a matter of a process of reasoning at all, but rather of some kind of blank commitment. Accordingly, the suggestion to which I now turn, that it is possible in principle for at least some moral rules to be ultimately vindicated, is likely to be greeted with a certain suspicion.

Let us consider first what is involved in accepting a moral rule, since the decision to do that is to be the conclusion of the reasoning we seek. The main point, of course, is that moral rules are rules of conduct. This implies that the man who has accepted a moral rule has in him a guide to conduct in the sense that the man who has accepted the rule to do A in C, if he finds himself in C, has in that fact a reason for doing A. That is, if he accepts the rule and comes to believe himself in C, then he has all the ingredients necessary for a piece of valid practical reasoning leading to the decision to do A. Moral rules make possible a reasoned transition from beliefs about circumstances to decisions on how to act.

Of course, there is more to a moral rule than the guidance of the conduct of the one who accepts it; in particular, there is the bearing of the rule on the conduct of others to whom the rule applies. This aspect of moral rules will be taken up at a later stage in the argument.

The claim that a moral rule in conjunction with information about circumstances leads to a decision to act may be challenged on the ground that surely it is possible for a person to accept a rule without acting on it. This possibility, I think, must be admitted; it is one form of weakness of will. But it is no objection to my claim. All I have said is that acceptance of the rule puts you into a position to reason from certain facts to certain decision to act. For a man to accept the facts and reject the decision would be irrational, just as it would be irrational for a man to accept that he is a man and that all men will die and yet reject the conclusion that he will die. In neither case does the irrationality of the thinking necessarily prevent it from occurring. To be sure, if a man displays this kind of weakness of will too frequently we will begin to doubt that he really does accept the rule. Similarly, if he too frequently displays a parallel kind of weakness of intellect by envisaging an unending future for himself, we will begin to doubt that he really does believe that all men will die. We assume that men are largely rational. Another more agonizing kind of weakness of will with a different diagnosis will concern us in a moment.

That moral rules guide conduct in the way specified can tell us something about what is required for their ultimate justification. Accepting a moral rule makes a demand on the will since it can sometimes require a decision to act even in the absence of other motivation. But logic does not give something for nothing. If the will is to be taxed in the conclusion it must be represented in the premises. This is the basic reason, I think, why moral rules cannot be ultimately validated; only a vindication which is carried on at the level of practical reason can allow the will a voice in the premises.

A vindication concludes in the decision to accept the rule. The full force of this may be obscured by a difficulty with the word "accept." We sometimes use this word simply to report the saying of Yes rather than No in a debate, and when we seek to go behind the words to the thought, we may suppose that accepting is an equally simple matter, a sort of mental saying of Yes rather than No. I am, however, using the word in a much more robust sense in which to accept a moral rule is to make oneself into the corresponding kind of man, a man who, among other things, manifests the regularity of generally doing what the rule requires. To get one's conduct to exhibit such a regularity, and to get oneself to fulfill any further conditions there may be of being an acceptor of the rule, may not be an easy task; in some cases it is very difficult, and in still others, perhaps, impossible. Great feats of self-discipline, will power and psychological trickery may be required. Smokers will appreciate this by reflecting on what would be involved in accepting the rule that one ought never to smoke.

The possibility of a second variety of weakness of will arises at this point. Suppose a man has an ultimate vindication of a certain moral rule. He reasons then to the decision to accept the rule. (Having this justification, he may even say "I *ought* to accept this rule," but this is the "ought" of reason, not the moral "ought," since his decision to accept the rule is not itself in obedience to any moral rule.) But even though he thus sets himself to the task of accepting the rule, he may fail; the task may be too difficult. We are likely to call a failure of this kind "weakness of will" because we feel that a man with a will of normal strength would be able to accomplish such a task through will power alone.

Of course, common experience teaches that will power is often not enough, and so the name may be something of a misnomer. Nor is will power the only method, since there are other techniques—hypnosis therapy, for example. On the other hand, there may be cases in which there is no way of bringing about acceptance of the rule. In such a case, that very fact shows the rule not to be vindicated after all. Vindications, being a species of practical reasoning, move in the sphere of the possible; a particular course of action, such as that of accepting a certain rule, cannot be the solution to the agent's practical problem if it is not open to him. Unfortunately, it is not easy to know in cases of this kind whether acceptance of the rule is really impossible, or whether it could be brought off with a little more effort. That is one reason why this kind of weakness of will often involves an element of anguish.

We now know something about the premises of an ultimate vindication and something about its conclusion; the next step is to enquire about the principle of practical reasoning leading from the one to the other. One familiar principle is, in Kantian terminology, that of "who wills the end wills the means." This principle permits a reasoned decision to do an action on the ground that it is the best means to an end that has been espoused.[3] We may begin by asking whether this principle can supply us with ultimate vindications of moral rules. I shall argue that, with a few exceptions, it cannot.

The main exception is that this principle does vindicate a rule for an agent who happens to have as an end some state of affairs for which acceptance of the rule is the best means. If a man just happens to want to be an honest man, then it might well be that accepting a moral rule about honesty would be the best means to this end, and that would vindicate acceptance of that rule. I shall call these *ideosyncratic* vindications on the ground that the desires on which they rest cannot be supposed to be widely shared—shared, that is, in a way that does not make the desire dependent on a prior acceptance of a moral rule. I shall set these vindications to one side for the present; at a later stage I shall argue that they do not vindicate their rules as *moral* rules.

If we consult the traditions of our subject, we find three main types of nonideosyncratic vindications employing the principle of who wills the end wills the means. These rest upon ends which we may characterize as love of God, love of self and love of man. For various reasons, I hold that none of these work. I shall not pause to rehearse the objections to a

---

3. I depart somewhat from the Kantian formula. Needless to say, the word "best" as used here is a carpet under which a lot of dirt is being swept.

religiously based ethics here. As to love of self, that is, the desire that I be happy, or that I get the most of what I will be glad to have gotten — vindications based on this founder on the difficulty that it does not seem to be the case that accepting moral rules is the best means to this end. It would seem that whatever you can get for yourself with a moral rule you could also get without it, and without it you could get even more.

It might be that some weird moral rule could be vindicated in this way — a "moral rule" of pure egoism, for example. Also, it must be admitted that this objection rests on contingent facts. If the world were made differently — if it were impossible for anyone ever to keep a secret because of universal telepathy, for example, then vindications of this type might become viable. My claim is that in the world as it is moral rules of the familiar kinds cannot be vindicated in this way.

Similar objections arise against a vindication based on the love of man, that is, the desire that men generally be happy. The vindications, presumably, would be that for a certain A and C, the general happiness requires the general doing of A in C. The only way to produce all this doing of A in C, it would be said, is for each person to accept the rule to do A in C. Thus, it would be claimed, the man who wants the general happiness to be maximized would have reason to accept the rule. Note that this proposed vindication relies on the idea that *everyone* is to accept the rule. I am supposed to reason: It would be good if everyone accepted the rule; my accepting the rule is a necessary, and hence part of the best, means to everyone accepting it; therefore, I must accept it. The trouble is that it is unrealistic to talk of *everybody* accepting the rule; there is bound to be at least one hold-out. To be realistic, I must think in terms of *general* acceptance, that is, acceptance by *most* persons. But once I thus allow the possibility of some persons not accepting the rule, then I must raise the question why I should not be one of them. My lust for the general happiness can be gratified if *most* people accept the rule. But this can mean most *other* people. And if *I* do not accept the rule, then that will leave me room to gratify some additional private lusts as well.

What about a pure act utilitarianism? This would be the "moral rule" to do A in C where C is "any situation" and A is "act having consequences in the circumstances most conducive to the general happiness." Presumably this rule would be vindicated for an agent because of the contribution *his* acceptance of it would make towards his end regardless of whether any others accepted it, and so the difficulties just raised would be overcome. But there are at least two objections. First, in view of human ignorance and folly, it is by no means clear that acceptance of such a rule would in fact be the best, or even a good, means to the proposed end. Second, it is by no means clear that "act having consequences in the circumstances most conducive to the general happiness" is a well-defined kind of act, at least with respect to every situation. In particular, it is not clear how this concept applies to situations involving my contribution to a complex cooperative action, where it is difficult to say of which contributing act the resulting situation is a consequence.

While these matters can and should be gone into in more detail, I am prepared at this point to draw at least the minimal conclusion that we should explore the possibility of some new principle or axiom of practical reasoning to replace or supplement the principle of who wills the end wills the means. To this task I now turn.

We may begin by picking up two loose ends left by the preceding discussion. One is the claim that an ideosyncratic vindication, even if successful in its own way, does not justify a moral rule as moral. The other is the complaint that while I have discussed how acceptance of a moral rule guides the conduct of the man who accepts it, I have said nothing about what his acceptance of the rule has to do with the conduct of others. These points are related, and the key lies in the two Kantian words "objectivity" and "universality." Morality is supposed to be objective; that is, it is not to depend on how things happen to be with this or that particular agent, but rather on how things must be with agents in general. That is why ideosyncratic vindications are out of place. Morality is also supposed to be universal; that is, everyone is included in the scope of its rules. So, when I accept a moral rule I not only acquire a guide for my own conduct; I also acquire a standard for judging the conduct of others. I do not think that we can hope for an adequate justification of moral rules unless these factors are brought in.

First, objectivity. Objectivity is a characteristic of thoughts, acts of thinking. I think objectively when I think in a way in which anyone would think—would think, that is, if his circumstances and condition were in the relevant respects ideal. More briefly, we may say that those thoughts are objective which everyone ideally-thinks.

A thought may be objective either absolutely or relatively to the thinker's situation. If the latter, then we say that anyone would ideally-think the same if in the same situation. If the former, then the thought is one that anyone would ideally-think in any situation or, what comes to the same thing, in the human situation as such. If, my hand being in the fire to no purpose, I will to have it out, that willing is presumably objective relative to my hand-in-fire situation. Anyone who in that situation willed differently would not be in that ideal condition in which what is ideally-thought is actually thought. And when I think that one and one is two, my thinking so is presumably objective absolutely.

There is another important distinction that applies in the case of thoughts that involve a reference to the thinker. My thought about myself is objective *in direct reference* if everyone ideally-thinks the same *about me.* It is objective *in parallel reference* if everyone ideally-thinks a parallel thought about himself. My belief that I am six-foot-two is objective in direct reference. My desire to have a fast car, if objective at all, is so only in parallel reference.

Now a word about the ideal conditions envisaged when we say that someone ideally-thinks something. This is best understood dialectically. A person ideally-thinks what he could be brought actually to think through a persistent, rational and sincere dialectic or debate which had available to it all methods of experiment and observation, and all other methods of rational persuasion. This includes some but not all techniques of self-discovery and attitude change. It is open to dialectic, for example, to bring a smoker into face to face contact with a person dying of lung cancer to see if he will continue to think that the pleasure of smoking is more important than health. But it is not open to dialectic to attach the smoker to a machine that gives him an electric shock every time he reaches for a cigarette.

Without staying to resolve the many difficulties with which these notions bristle, let us rush ahead to the point that some modes of thought presuppose objectivity in various senses. "Presuppose" here means that the thinker of the thought cannot rationally believe that his thought lacks objectivity in the relevant sense. Factual belief, for example, presupposes absolute objectivity in direct reference.

The decision to accept a moral rule presupposes absolute objectivity in parallel reference. I cannot rationally decide to make myself an acceptor of a moral rule while at the same time thinking that some do not ideally-decide to accept the same rule themselves. This is part of the meaning of the word "moral," or of one of its meanings, and is what marks off morality from such things as personal choice of life-style, the custom of particular groups, and so on.

This presupposition of objectivity in parallel reference of the decision to accept the rule gives rise to a presupposition of objectivity in direct reference of any moral judgment based on the rule. This is a consequence of the other Kantian feature, universality. When I judge the conduct of another I do so on the basis of my moral rules, which apply to him because they are universal in scope. My decision to accept my moral rule, however, presupposes that he ideally-decides to accept the same rule, and hence that he ideally makes the same judgment about his own conduct, or that of anyone else. It is thus presupposed that everyone ideally makes the same moral judgments about anyone's conduct, and this amounts to objectivity in direct reference of the moral judgment.

Something like this, I believe, is the proper account of the bearing of my acceptance of a moral rule on the conduct of others. When I judge others, I do so with a presupposition of objectivity. But that is all. I need not be telling them what to do, nor advising them, nor seeking to guide their conduct in any way.[4] This view has the advantage that we can retain the conception of morality as a machinery for guiding conduct without converting it into an engine of persuasion. The persuading, if done at all, is done by the dialectic through which we may seek to bring others actually to think what they ideally-think.

We are not in a position to examine the bearing of all this on the issue of the ultimate vindication of moral rules. The chief lesson to be learned, I think, is that if we are to vindicate a moral rule as moral, then the vindication must also show the objectivity of the rule. And this in turn requires that all premisses of the vindication be objective. If everyone ideally-accepts all the premisses of a valid piece of reasoning, then everyone ideally-accepts the conclusion, and so such a vindication (and, I think, such a vindication alone) will guarantee the objectivity of the acceptance of the moral rule.

These considerations also *suggest* what is required by way of a practical assumption in addition to the principle of who wills the end wills the means. I shall call it the *will to objectivity*. It is the universalized conditional decision actually to think a thing if one ideally-thinks it. Though the effect of such a decision is clear — that I will that I think in a certain way as soon as I come to believe that I ideally-think in that way — its logical form is obscure. The obscurity touches both the respect in which the decision is conditional and that in which it is universalized. I shall not attempt to dispel these clouds at this time. Instead, I shall represent the special kind of conditionality involved by a horseshoe, the universality by prefixed universal quantifier, and shall lay down a couple of rules which these devices are assumed to obey. Accordingly, I express the will to objectivity as:

$$(m)(p)\$(I\ m\text{-think}^i\ p \supset I\ m\text{-think}\ p)$$

Here, "m" indicates a mode of thought, "p" a content, "i" means "ideally," and "$\$$" indicates an expression of practical decision. As to rules, I shall first assume that the usual quantifier laws apply. Thus, from the above I can move, for example, to the particular conditional decision to desire that I be honest if I ideally-desire that I be honest. That is,

$$\$(I\ desire^i\ that\ I\ am\ honest \supset I\ desire\ that\ I\ am\ honest)$$

And I assume a second rule which permits a *modus ponens* like move from a conditional decision and the affirmation of its antecedent to the decision to realize its consequent. Thus from the above, together with

---

4. Such 'dynamic' accounts of other directed moral judgments have been vigorously and effectively attacked by Charles Baylis in "Grading, Values, and Choice," *Mind*, no. 10 (1958), 485–501.

I desire[i] that I am honest,

I may reason to

$(I desire that I am honest),

which expressed my decision to make myself into a person who desires to be honest.

And I shall assume that the will to objectivity is itself objective, at least in parallel reference. And on this assumption I shall conclude this paper by presenting in a very schematic way a possible logical form for the ultimate justification of a moral rule which rests on the will to objectivity, which is not wholly implausible, which, if successful, guarantees the objectivity of the moral rule it vindicates, and which whatever its flaws, at least has the advantage of showing us the kinds of assumptions that might need to be made if a moral rule is to be justified.

The pivot of this vindication is the claim that there is an objective end — absolutely objective with direct reference: that is, that there is something that everyone ideally-wills. There are many conceivable objective ends to be considered. For example, there may be a being so excellent that everybody ideally-wills that the wishes of this being be fulfilled, and this might be the foundation of certain moral rules. Instead of this, however, I shall follow J. S. Mill (more or less) and seek to establish the general happiness as an example of an objective end. That is, I will try to show that everyone ideally-wills that everyone be happy.

We begin with the assumption of hedonism.

(1) (Assumption of Hedonism) Everyone ideally-wills that he himself be happy.

$(x)(x$ wills[i] that x is happy$)$

This expresses the idea that the happiness of each person is a good to that person. The task is to make plausible a transition from this to the view that the general happiness is a good to the aggregate of persons. This second idea may be restated as the claim that there is a group of which everyone is a member and which, as a group, ideally-wills that everyone be happy.

We are thus led to the difficult notion of a group ideally-willing something. What a group ideally-wills is presumably what the group could be brought actually to will through dialectic. This in turn brings in the notion of a group actually willing something. Both of these notions are very obscure. For the group to come to will something through dialectic is presumably for the group to carry through perfectly some ideal group decision-making process. What such a process would be like is not easy to say. But it seems plausible to hold that if through such a process a group could come to will anything at all, it would come to will that each member get what he ideally-wants. And this seems all the more plausible when each member ideally-wants the same thing. So I shall assume that this is true about group ideal-willing and call it the assumption of common purpose. Accordingly, we have:

(2) (Assumption of Common Purpose) If every member of a group ideally-wills that he have a certain thing, then the group ideally-wills that every member have that thing.
  $(g)[(x)(x$ belongs to $g \supset x$ wills^i that $\phi x) \supset g$ wills^i that $(x)(x$ belongs to $g \supset \phi x)]$

Let us now add the slightly less daunting assumption that the aggregate of persons does form a group.

(3) (Assumption of the Universal Group) There is a group to which everyone belong.
  $(\exists g)(x)(x$ belongs to $g)$

From these assumptions we may move to the desired conclusion concerning the general happiness and the aggregate of persons.

(4) (From 1, 2 and 3) There is a group to which everyone belongs and which ideally-wills that everyone be happy.
  $(\exists g)[(x)(x$ belongs to $g)$ & g wills^i that $(x)(x$ is happy$)]$

The next step is to transform this group ideal-willing of the general happiness into an individual ideal-willing of it. The mediating link is the notion of solidarity with a group. We assume that, ideally, individuals maintain solidarity with the groups of which they are members with respect to group goals.

(5) (Assumption of Goal Solidarity) An individual who is a member of a group that ideally-wills that p ideally-wills that p himself.
  $(x)[(\exists g)(x$ belongs to g & g wills^i $p) \supset x$ wills^i $p]$

We may then move directly to the general happiness as an objective end.

(6) (From 4 and 5) Everyone ideally-wills the happiness of everyone.
  $(x)[x$ wills^i that $(y)(y$ is happy$)]$

We may now turn to the second half of the vindication, which seeks to carry us from an objective end to a moral rule. Here the inspiration comes from Kant rather than Mill. I shall present the argument in general terms, setting aside the fact that the objective end we have established is that of the general happiness, and assuming only that we have agreed upon some objective end or other, which I shall label *e*. Accordingly, we begin the second half with

> (7) (Assumption of the Objective End) Everyone ideally-wills that *e*.
> *(x)(x* wills*ⁱ* that *e)*

It is necessary next to relate the rule *R*, to do *A* in *C*, to *e* as a means. This relation, of course, has to do with acceptance of *R*, and in fact, acceptance by the universal group. So we assume that group acceptance of *R* is the best means to *e*.

> (8) (Assumption of the Utility of *R*) *e* requires as best means that there be a group which has everyone as a member and which accepts *R*.
> *e* m⊃ *(∃g)((x)(x* belongs to *g)* & *g* accepts *R)*

The concept of group acceptance of a rule is no easier than that of group willing considered above. For it to be said that a group accepts *R* it is necessary that large numbers of the members of the group accept *R*. It is perhaps also necessary that most members of the group know that *R* is widely accepted so that there can be a general expectation of conformity to R. It is perhaps even necessary that there be some kind of group sanction enforcing conformity to *R*, though this is less clear.

People, ideally, reason in accordance with the principles of practical reason, and so, in view of the principle of who wills the end wills the means, we may move on to:

> (9) (From 7 and 8) Everyone ideally-wills that there be a group having everyone as a member which accepts *R*.
> (x)[x wills that *(∃g)((y)(y* belongs to *g)* & *g* accepts *R)*]

In order to make the transition from this to individual acceptance of the rule we must exploit another aspect of the notion of solidarity with a group, which I shall call Rule Solidarity. One has this kind of solidarity with a group when one wills to accept oneself those rules which one wills the group to accept. The assumption we require is that such solidarity, at least with those groups of which one wills to be a member, is objective (absolutely, with parallel reference). That is, we have:

> (10) (Assumption of Rule Solidarity) If one wills that there be a group such that one belongs to it and it accepts *R*, then one ideally-wills to accept *R* oneself.
> *(x)[(x* wills that *(∃g)(x* belongs to *g* & *g* accepts *R))* ⊃ *x* wills*ⁱ* that *x* accepts *R*]

Now it seems clear that if one ideally-thinks in manner *A*, and if it is also true that if one actually thought in manner *A* then one would ideally-think in manner *B*, then it follows that one ideally-thinks in manner *B*.

This principle concerning the logic of ideal-thinking carries us from (9) and (10) to:

(11) (From 9 and 10) Everyone ideally-wills that he accepts R.
$(x)(x$ wills^i that x accepts $R)$

And then, instantiating this for my own case, I reach

(12) (From 11) I ideally-will to accept R.
I will^i that I accept R

It is now time to make use of the will to objectivity. By reasoning based on it of the sort considered above, I may move from (12) to

(13) (From 12 and Will to Objectivity) It shall be that I will that I accept R)
$\$(I$ will that I accept $R)$

As I have argued elsewhere,[5] if an ideally rational being wills to will something, then he wills it. This principle of the logic of volition takes me from (13) to

(14) (From 13 and Logic of Volition) It shall be that I accept R.
$\$(I$ accept $R)$

Which concludes the ultimate vindication of R.

The above demonstration is only meant to be suggestive of the kind of logical foundation upon which moral rules must rest, if they are to rest on any at all, and I make no claim that it is in any way definitive. But it does seem to me that certain features of it will need to be present in any acceptable justification. These are, first, the form of a vindication. Second, the reliance on the will to objectivity, and still more, the concept of objectivity and the contrast between ideal and actual thinking. Third, the establishing of an objective end, and of the conduciveness of the moral rule to it. Fourth, the concept of a group, and of groups ideally and actually deciding, accepting rules, etc. And finally, the idea of individual solidarity with a group.

Some or all of these may be shams and illusions. In that event, if I am right, moral rules will have no ultimate justification, and rational men will look for alternatives to them.

5. In "A Theory of Practical Reason," cited above.

Goodness, Intentions, and Propositions

Hector-Neri Castañeda

Indiana University

Dedication. This essay is dedicated to Charles Baylis, an authentic and generous friend, who has seriously, and quite properly, worried both about the nature of propositions and about the nature of goodness.

Conventions. Single quotes around words, phrases or sentences form, as usual, names of the words, phrases, or sentences so surrounded. Double quotation marks around a sentence or phrase form a name of some proposition, or propositional function, or entity, here not specified, formulatable by the sentence or phrase in question on some occasion. We simply assume that there are methods for determining for each occasion what property or propositional function is expressed with a given sentence.

The terms 'state of affairs', 'proposition', and 'statement' will be taken to refer to the same type of entity. The first is the most neutral and objective one; the second puts the slant on propositions being possible contents of psychological acts or attitudes, while the third puts the slant on propositions being the contexts of linguistic acts. Naturally, in adopting this convention I am adopting the use of the phrases 'true state of affairs' and 'false state of affairs'. These are rare usages, I concede.

Introduction

At the heart of this essay is the view that axiological concepts (or properties, if you wish) must be sharply distinguished from deontic concepts (or properties). This is a familiar thesis, defended in this century by H. A. Prichard[1] and by William David Ross.[2] But the argument de-

An early version of this paper was presented at a Philosophy faculty colloquium of the University of Cincinnati in November of 1970. I have benefited from comments made on that version by Romane Clark, Charles Daniels, Paul Eisenberg, Jack Meiland, and Rollin Workman. I am also grateful to Elizabeth Myers for many stylistic and grammatical improvements.

1. H. A. Prichard, "Does Moral Philosophy Rest on a Mistake?" *Mind,* ns, 21 (1912), reprinted in H. A. Prichard, *Moral Obligation* (Oxford, England: Clarendon Press, 1949), and in many anthologies.

2. W. D. Ross, *The Right and the Good* (Oxford, England: Clarendon Press, 1930), ch. 1.

ployed here is entirely different from the arguments of other philosophers who have attacked the problem. As far as I know, it is a novel argument, one which has tantalized successive classes of students who have taken my course in Twentieth Century Ethical Theories.

It may be useful to formulate our problem within a framework of more general problems about goodness (and badness). To begin with, entities of all kinds and categories are said, and often correctly said, to be good or bad. We attribute goodness to material things, as, for instance, when we judge

(A.1)   This is a good steak.

We predicate goodness of actions, as in

(B.1)   A good thing to do is to wait for Smith.

We attribute goodness to persons, as when we say

(C.1)   John is a good student,

or

(C.2)   John is a good man.

We attribute goodness to properties or qualities, as in

(D.1)   This wine has some excellent features (or good qualities).

We attribute goodness to states of affairs or propositions, as in

(E.1)   It was good that John came.

We predicate goodness of intentions, for instance:

(F.1)   John's intention to come was good.

And to make things more perplexing, we also *seem* to predicate value *relations* of agents and actions or states of affairs. Thus, while in the preceding examples goodness appears to be a monadic or nonrelational property, in the following examples goodness appears to be a *relation* between a person and a state of affairs (or proposition) or an action:

(G.1)   It was good of John to come;
(H.1)   It was good of John that he came;
(J.1)   It was good for Smith that John came.

The varied uses of the word 'good' raise a battery of interesting problems concerning the nature of the word 'good' and the nature of the concepts goodness, badness and value in general. Whether the words 'good' and 'bad' are used to predicate properties or not, as some philosophers would have it, the fundamental fact is that these words occur in a bewildering diversity of syntactico-semantical constructions, as was illustrated above. These constructions need accounting for. Whatever metaphysical view one holds about values, the fact is that goodness and badness appear to consciousness, in thoughts about values, as properties of some sort. A detailed description of the phenomenology of such apparent properties is both an unavoidable task of philosophical elucidation, and a prerequisite test for the adequacy of any reductionist theory that is to analyze away the propertyhood of goodness and badness. Thus, we feel justified methodologically in adopting an ostensibly objective formulation or posture, for the purpose of phenomenological description.

To the extent that goodness appears as a property in the examples (A.1) through (J.1), we face questions like: (I) Is one and the same property predicated variously by the adjective 'good', crossing over logical ranks, or are there several different properties? (II) If several properties are predicated with the adjective 'good', is one of them primary, the others being analyzable in terms of it? (III) Is the primary goodness a property of states of affairs or propositions, or is it a property of properties? (IV) Is there more than one primary goodness? How many more? In another paper[3] I have argued that: (A) The goodness of properties is derivative: properties are good in the sense that they make states of affairs or propositions good; (B) the goodness of particulars is also derivative: it is analyzable in terms of the goodness(es) and badness(es) of states of affairs; (C) states of affairs or propositions are the ultimate subjects of value predication. In that essay I did not, however, consider apparently relational or relative value judgments like (F.1), "John's intention to come was good," (G.1), "It was good of John to come," and (J.1), "It was good for Smith that John came." Although I defended view (C), that states of affairs are the ultimate or primary value subjects, I did not proceed far enough to submit an answer to question (IV), whether there is more than one primary goodness. Here I propose to move closer to an answer to question (IV). I want to continue that investigation by inquiring into the difference between (E.1), "It is good that John came," and (G.1), "It was good of John to come."

In this essay I will attempt to establish two phenomenological theses: (D) there are at least two primary and irreducible goodnesses; (E) one goodness applies to states of affairs (or propositions), the other to intentions and, more generally, to prescriptions. Part of the paper will develop the contrast between propositions and intentions. This is a special case

---

3. "On the Ultimate Subjects of Value Predication," in John W. Davis, ed., *Value and Valuation. Axiological Studies in Honor of Robert S. Hartman* (Knoxville: University of Tennessee Press, 1971).

of the contrast between propositions and prescriptions, which I have discussed at some length in earlier papers.[4]

Strictly speaking, neither goodness is really a property; one is an operator on propositions, and the other is an operator on intentions and prescriptions. That is to say, in "It is good that John came" we have a proposition resulting from the proposition "John came" by the "action" of the operator or connector expressed with the syntactical prefix 'it is good that'. In 'It is good that John came' the word 'good' does not function as an adjective "modifying" a noun naming the proposition that John came. The word 'good' *does* function in that way in the sentence ' "John came" is good'. And we must indeed distinguish very sharply between the second-order propositions (if any) expressible with the latter sentence from the corresponding ones expressible with the sentence 'It is good that John came'. Similar considerations hold, mutatis mutandis, for 'It was good of John to come'. But we shall not go into this matter here. We shall sometimes speak of value properties or of goodness as a property, for convenience, to conform to tradition, using the term 'property' in a wider sense, without in the least implying that, in a narrower and preferable sense of 'property', operators are better conceived of as non-properties.

I. *Enter Intentions*

As ordinary psychological and axiological vocabularies are so complex and baffling, it is not altogether unnatural that a person may on occasion use the following two sentences to make exactly the same statement:

(E.1)   It was good that John came,

and

(G.1)   It was good of John to come.

Yet a simple reflection on the conventions of English reveals that it is more appropriate and natural for such sentences to be used to make two quite different statements, differing in the role each assigns to the agent John. While (E.1) bestows value on the state of affairs "John came" as a whole, (G.1) bestows a special value, or so it seems, on John. Let these sentences, therefore, be used in their more natural way, and suppose that in (E.1) and (G.1) above we have two statements.

4. Especially in "Actions, Imperatives, and Obligations," *Aristotelian Society Proceedings,* 68 (1967–68), 25–48. See also H. N. Castañeda, *The Structure of Morality* (Springfield, Ill.: Charles Thomas Publisher, 1974), chs. 2–5.

Clearly, statement (G.1) is not equivalent to statement (E.1). Indeed, neither one implies the other. It may well be a good thing that John happens to be at the place in question, to have made the successful effort of being there, and yet it may fail to be good of him; indeed, it may be palpably bad of him to come because of what he *intended* to do, whether he accomplished his evil intention or not. That is, (E.1) can be true while (G.1) is false, so that (E.1) does not imply (G.1). Likewise, it may be a bad thing that John came, though it was good of him to have come, because of what he intended to do. That is, (G.1) does not, in its turn, imply (E.1).

The nonequivalence above suggests that (F.1) might be analyzable as:

(G.1.b)   John came and it was good that he intended to come.

It may be thought that (G.1.b) is not strong enough in that the point of asserting (G.1) may be to praise a man not simply for being in the state of having the intention to come, but for having reached the state of intending *after deliberation*. Thus, (G.1) is to be analyzed, according to this suggestion, as

(G.1.c)   John came and it was (is) good that he decided to come.[5]

Perhaps, as indicated above, it is not uncommon for a person to use sentence (G.1) to make a statement that could properly be expressed with sentence (G.1.c). Yet the semantical conventions of the language seem to make another statement more fittingly expressible by means of sentence (G.1). It seems to me that neither (G.1.b) nor (G.1.c) can do as formulations of that more fitting statement. It may be the case that John intended to do something or other, simply because it is good that he has the ability to frame intentions (or decisions), or because it is, in general, good that there are beings who can intend (or decide). Yet it may at the same time be bad of him to come, because his *intention* (or decision) to come is itself bad. That is, for (G.1) to be true it is required that the *contents* of John's intending (or deciding) be good, but it is not required that he perform a good act of intending (or deciding) or that he be in a good state of intending (or deciding). Thus, the analysis of (G.1) is more likely the following:

(G.1.d)   John came and his intention to come was good.

I will drop the references to decisions, since a decision is an intention arrived at after a process of deliberation.

It seems that statement

(G.2)   It was good of John that he came,

5. I am indebted for this suggestion to Romane Clark.

is the same statement as (G.1). Hence, it seems also to be the same as the conjunction (G.1.d). The first conjunct, the factual "John came" is at any rate a part and parcel of (G.1) and (G.2). This is clearly indicated by the categorical indicative past tense.

Statement (G.1) is clearly praiseful of John. And it may be thought that part of the statement is that John has a lot to do with the goodness of his coming qua event in the world. That is to say, it may be thought that part of statement (G.1) is that John's coming resulted from John's intention to come.[6] I am persuaded that this proposition is part of the statement one often means to assert when using sentence (G.1). But I am inclined to think that such a statement is more perspicuously put thus:

(G.3)   It was good of John that he came intentionally,

or as:

(G.4)   It was good of John that he came as a result of his intending to come.[7]

I shall not provide here a full analysis of proposition (G.1). It suffices for my present purpose that an analysis like (G.1.d) provides the fundamental schema. According to it, (G.1) is to be analyzed as a conjunction of some propositions, one conjunct of which is "John's intention to come was good." *This schema has the merit of reducing the apparently relational goodness of (G.1) to the goodness of an intention*, a goodness which we must in any case reckon with.

Now the question is: What are intentions, i.e., what are the contents of intending? In particular, we must ask: Are intentions propositions? If intentions are propositions, then by (G.1.c) we can claim that the relational goodness that holds between agents and their actions is reducible to the goodness of propositions. On the other hand, if intentions are not propositions, then we have to investigate independently whether the goodness of intentions is the same property as the goodness of propositions. (It is a mistake to conclude automatically that the goodness of intentions is different from the goodness of propositions, just because propositions and intentions are different entities.)

II. *Intentions, Propositions and Prescriptions*

Statement (G.1.d) is a conjunction, and each conjunct is a proposition or statement (remember that we are using these two words to refer to

6. I owe this suggestion to Charles Daniels.
7. I owe the examples (G.3) and (G.4), as well as the idea of their equivalence, to Jack Meiland.

the same entities). Both "John came" and "John's intention to come was good" are propositions, for (i) each one of them is either true or false, and (ii) each of them can be believed by a person. Our interest focuses on the last conjunct of (G.1.d):

(F.1)   John's intention to come was good.

Our problem is to pin down the entity which according to (F.1) possesses goodness. In order to work up an answer let us note that the word 'intention' functions as a signal *from outside* proposition (F.1), so to speak, of the kind of entity which possesses goodness according to (F.1). Similarly, the genitive case of the name 'John' merely indicates that the entity which is the intention has John as a constituent: This genitive is a signal of the copulation of subject and predicate, as when we say "John's color" or "John's humanity." Thus, I submit that the infinitive clause:

(John) . . . to come

as it is used within the sentence 'John's intention to come was good' presents the entity which is the intention and which is the possessor of goodness according to (F.1). It is indeed the same clause that both appears in 'It was good of *John to come*' and formulates the same intention which is a constituent of statement (G.1). The tantalizing feature of (G.1) lies in that the *same* infinitive clause, in the context of sentence (G.1), *also* formulates the proposition "John came." It is this double role that makes it initially somewhat plausible to claim that (G.1) is the same statement as (G.2), in which goodness appears to be a relation between John and the proposition "John came." But, if (G.2) is the same as (G.1), then we must distinguish in the clause 'he (John) came' appearing in the context of the sentence 'It was good of John that he came' two different roles: (i) that of formulating the proposition "John came," which is entailed by both (G.1) and (G.2), and (ii) the role of formulating the intention which possesses goodness. In either case, we still have to determine whether or not an intention (in the present sense) is a proposition.

Let us congeal some terminology in order to avoid some confusions. The word 'intention' is here being used to refer to the "content," or "object" if you wish, of a state of intending. Thus, while intending is a practical counterpart of believing, intentions are the corresponding counterparts of propositions. It is not a mere accident that the word 'intention' is used with the same type of ambiguity that infects the use of the word 'belief'. But both words are more typically used to refer to thought contents, not to states of minds. Similarly, just as the same proposition can be a belief, a conjecture, a supposition, a premise, or a conclusion, likewise the same practical content can be an intention or a decision.

Let us take a closer look at the intention presented by the sentence

(F.1)   John's intention to come was good.

This intention, which is the content of an act or attitude of intending on John's part, is a decision that he would, or in fact did, express by saying, perhaps only to himself, "I will come." Intentions are first-person thought contents, so that in order to present another man's intentions for consideration by a third party we need some linguistic machinery that both (i) presents a first-person reference, and (ii) relates that reference to its owner or maker. In the sentence 'John's intention to come was good' the word intention performs role (i) and the possessive noun 'John's' performs role (ii). Thus, given our convention at the beginning of the paper concerning quotation marks, the structure of the nominal phrase 'John's intention to come' seems to have essentially the same role as our double quotation marks. That is, the nominal phrase 'John's intention to come' seems to mean the same as 'John's intention "I will come" '.

Now if there are implicit double quotation marks in 'John's intention to come', then statement (G.1.d), "John came and his intention to come was good," is not really the analysis of our paradigm

(G.1)   It was good of John to come.

This latter statement does not have any built in quotes, nor does it predicate of any intention that it is an intention. To put it differently, on the above double-quotation analysis of 'John's intention to come', statement (G.1.d) is a second-order statement *about* an intention, while (G.1) is a first-order statement *built from* an intention. But the discussion has brought out the structure of (G.1): it is the application of an operator "It is good that" to an intention of John's, not to a statement that John has such and such an intention, and not to the conception of that intention.

There is, however, no obvious and ready way in ordinary English to exhibit my structural analysis of (G.1) so as to remove John from the operator, and, of course, also leave John out of the intention in question. This intention has, not John himself, but John's first-person reference as a constituent. We can, certainly, invent a special notation. We may use the name 'John' as a mere signal that represents John's intentions *in viva persona* by putting it as a subscript of first-person future-tense sentences. Thus, in our example we have the sentence '$[(I$ will come at $T')_{John, T}]$' that can represent John's intention at T' that he has decided upon at time T. With this machinery, we can represent our paradigm

(G.1)   It was good of John to come

more perspicuously as:

(G.1*)   For some times T and T': It is good [(I will come at T')$_{John, T}$] and T was earlier than, or simultaneous with, T', and T' was before now, and John came at T'.

Patently, (G.1*) is more perspicuous in five respects: (i) it separates the propositional component "John came" from the intentional one; (ii) it disentangles the time relationships built around the past tense 'was' and the infinitive 'to come'; (iii) it shows that we are not dealing with a relational, but only with a monadic, goodness; (iv) it exhibits the role of John in the whole set-up as a mere *coordinate* determining an intention; and (v) it reveals the first-order character of our paradigm. All of these structural features are, therefore, beautifully compacted in the ordinary-language construction 'it was good of John to come'.

Now, *intentions are not propositions, since:* (1) *intentions lack truth-values, and* (2) *intentions are not objects of, or units of content of, belief.* Intending is analogous to believing, but different from it in that it takes intentions, not propositions, as its objects. Belief, in its most customary sense, is a disposition or propensity which is (pace the behaviorists) exercised in acts of thinking that such and such is the case. Likewise, intending is, in its most customary sense, a disposition or propensity which is exercised in acts of deciding, and in affirmations or rehearsals of decisions. But unlike believing, intending is not a purely intellectual propensity, but a propensity that exercises practical reason: it rearranges the motivational or causal routes constitutive at the time in question of the person whose intending it is. At the moment, however, we are not interested in the rational psychology of action. Our concern is with the logic and ontology of the objects of intending. Note, however, that the word 'think' is often used neutrally with respect to the purely cognitive and the practico-cognitive. Thus, it is correct to say that beliefs, or believings, are exercised in acts of thinking, and also that intendings (or intentions, in the sense of "act," not object) are exercised in acts of thinking. But while the former are thinkings-that, the latter are, rather, thinkings-to: e.g., "Jones was thinking to come."

There is a third difference between propositions and intentions, namely: (3) *intentions are not conditions,* necessary or sufficient; they cannot be formulated by clauses which are subordinated to conditioning particles, like 'if', 'provided that', 'only if', etc. An intention is often formulated by means of a future-tense sentence. For example, a man may make a decision by saying "I will come tomorrow." His decision, an intention, differs from his prediction that he will come, a proposition, in that: (1) it lacks a truth-value, and (2) it is not an object of his belief. On the other hand, if the man says "If I will come tomorrow, then . . .", the future-tense clause following his utterance of the word 'if' will not formulate a decision. The clause will formulate a proposition which is claimed by the speaker to be a sufficient condition of fact for whatever is formulated in the consequent of his conditional assertion, and this consequent may, of course, very well be an intention.

Feature (3) is important, because some philosophers have spoken of statements or propositions that have no truth-value. But even if the lack of truth-values were not sufficient to establish that intentions are not species of propositions, characteristics (2) and (3) do bring this out forcefully.

Lacking truth-values is, however, crucial for intentions. If a proposition P does not have a truth-value, then either (a) its denial Not-P has a truth-value or (b) it does not. In case (a), we can still distinguish propositions from intentions by means of truth-values because the denial of an intention, which is itself an intention also lacks a truth-value. In case (b), either (b.1) the proposition which is the disjunction of P and Not-P is a tautology and has the value truth; or (b.2) that disjunction does not have the value truth. In case (b.1), intentions and propositions are different entities, since the disjunction of an intention and its denial is tautologous, but it is not true. Non-truth-valued thought contents like intentions and commands are tautologous when they have the form of a truth-table tautology.[8] In case (b.2), there is a disjunction of P and Not-P and some other proposition, perhaps, Not-not-P such that the three-membered disjunction is true, logically true. On the other hand, if intentions were three-valued, their tautological disjunctions would be true. But intentions are *absolutely* lacking in truth-values: no connective compound of intentions has a truth-value.

Intentions are first-person contents of practical thought. When the thought in question is an act of thinking it is an act of deciding or rehearsing a previously reached decision. When the thought in question is dispositional, i.e., a propensity to rehearse decisions and to perform the acts presented in those decisions, the propensity is an attitude of intending or having an intention. But the thought contents are the same: first-person non-truth-valued contents expressible with sentences of the form 'I will A' or 'I shall do A', depending on the speaker's dialect.[9]

Intentions or decisions (as thought contents, that is) belong with pieces of advice, requests, orders and the contents of assertive and deliberate

8. For further arguments for the cleavage between propositions and intentions see my "Intentions and the Structure of Intending," *The Journal of Philosophy,* 68 (1971), 453–466, and my "Intentions and Intending," *American Philosophical Quarterly,* 9 (1972), 139–149.

9. For a detailed and formal argument in defense of the two-valued structure of the logic of commands see my "On the Semantics of the Ought-to-Do," *Synthese,* 21 (1970), 449–468. For a parallel argument for intentions see my "Intentions and Intending," mentioned in footnote 8.

acts of telling a person what to do. I have used before[10] the term *'mandate'* as the generic term to group all the contents of such acts, and the term *'prescription'* to refer to the structure common to a family of mandates that demand of the same agents the doing of the same actions in exactly the same circumstances. For example, the order "Peter, go home," the request "Peter, please go home," and the advice "Peter, do go home" (uttered in the appropriate tone of voice), assuming, of course, that we have the same Peter and the same time throughout, have as underlying structure the prescription "Peter go home" — expressed clearly by the absence of the customary imperative-denoting comma after 'Peter'. I will call the class of prescriptions and intentions *practitions*. Intentions are first-person practitions. They are the first-person counterparts of mandates. But they are *not* first-person mandates.[11] The fundamental contrast we are dealing with is not that between intentions and propositions, but that between practitions and propositions.

III. *Two Types of Goodness*

We have, then, two types of entity which are conceived of as good: propositions and intentions. Now our pressing question becomes: Is the goodness of a proposition the same property (or operator) as the goodness of an intention? Or do we have two different properties (or operators)? From the mere fact that intentions are not propositions it does not follow that the property ascribed to intentions by means of the adjective 'good' or, rather, the operator 'it is good', is different from the property ascribed to propositions by means of the same adjective, or operator. I do not have any really knockdown argument to prove that the answer must be affirmative, or that it must be negative. But I have an argument which, I believe, strongly supports the claim that the goodness of intentions is a different property (or operator) from the goodness of propositions. I proceed to discuss it. Consider, first, the following proposition:

10. See the paper mentioned in footnote 4, as well as "On the Semantics of the Ought-To-Do" mentioned in footnote 9; and "Imperatives, Decisions, and Oughts: A Logico-Metaphysical Investigation," in H-N. Castañeda and G. Nakhnikian (eds.), *Morality and the Language of Conduct* (Detroit: Wayne State University Press, 1963).

11. For problems relating to demonstrative or indexical reference and for a defense of the view that first-person propositions are irreducible to second- and third-person propositions see my essays "Indicators and Quasi-Indicators," *American Philosophical Quarterly*, 4, no. 2 (April, 1967), 85–100; "On the Logic of Attributions of Self-Knowledge to Others," *The Journal of Philosophy*, 65, no. 15 (Aug. 1968), 439–456, and "On the Phenomeno-logic of the I," *Proceedings of the XIVth International Congress of Philosophy* (Vienna: Herber, 1968), III, 260–266.

(G.11)   It will be good of Jones to do the following: to apologize to Smith by letter unless the mailmen go on a strike.

It seems perfectly clear that (G.11) is equivalent to, even if not identical with, the proposition:

(G.11.a)   Unless the mailmen go on a strike, it will be good of Jones to apologize to Smith by letter.

The interesting thing about this equivalence is that, while in (G.11), goodness is ascribed to the disjunctive intention "Jones . . . to apologize to Smith unless the mailmen go on a strike" *as a whole,* in (G.11.a) goodness is ascribed only to the disjunct "Jones . . . to apologize to Smith by letter." On the other hand,

(G.12)   It will be good of Jones to apologize to Smith by letter or to apologize by wire.

is *not* equivalent to, and, a fortiori, *not* identical with

(G.12.a′) (Either) Jones apologizes (will apologize) to Smith by letter, or it will be good of Jones to apologize to Smith by wire.

Similarly, (G.12) is not equivalent to

(G.12.a″) (Either) Jones apologizes (will apologize) to Smith by wire, or it will be good of Jones to apologize to Smith by letter.

On the other hand, (G.12) is equivalent to, even though not identical with,

(G.12.a)   (Either) it will be good of Jones to apologize to Smith by letter, or it will be good of Jones to apologize to Smith by wire.

The preceding examples illustrate and, hence, provide evidence for, the following principles, where '*p*' stands for propositions and '*i*' for intentions:

I.1.   A connective compound having a proposition as one component and an intention as the other component is an intention.
GI.2.   "It is good of X that *(p or i)*" is equivalent to "*p* or it is good of X that *i*."

Now, in full parallelism with GI.2 we have:

GP.2.   "It is good that *(p or q)*" is equivalent to "It is good that *p* or it is good that *q*."

Obviously, a principle that governs both propositions and intentions is this, where '*$*p*' and '*$*q*' stand for propositions or intentions, as needed:

GPI.3′. If *p is equivalent to *q, then "It is good that *p" is equivalent to "It is good that *q."

By 'equivalence' I mean, of course, logical coimplication in the sense required for the logic of intentions and the logic of value properties or operators. Obviously, equivalence is not identity.

The above principles help in the construction of a preliminary argument in support of the view that the goodness of intentions is a different property (or operator) from the goodness of propositions. Here we assume that the logic of intentions is two-valued and parallel to the logic of propositions. I have argued for this position in detail elsewhere.[12] *Suppose*, then, that the goodness of propositions is identical with the goodness of intentions, and consider the following deduction, where equivalence is represented by a double arrow, and quotation marks and Quine's corners are both left implicit:

1. $p \leftrightarrow p \lor (p \,\&\, i)$ tautology
2. It is good $(p) \leftrightarrow$ It is good $(p \lor (p \,\&\, i))$ by GPI.3′
3. It is good $(p) \leftrightarrow p \lor$ it is good $(p \,\&\, i)$ by GI.2

Clearly, 3 is false. It may very well be the case that p is true, though both neither p nor $p \,\&\, i$ are good. More specifically, from 3 it follows that "It is good that p, if p," that is, every realized state of affairs is good. This is clearly false.

A reply to the preceding argument is that principle GPI.3′ needs a restriction:

GPI.2. If *p and *q are equivalent and are either both propositions or both intentions, then "It is good (*p)" is equivalent to "It is good (*q)."

Thus we can block the step from 2 to 3 in the preceding deduction.

Now, it is natural to suppose that the goodness which applies to propositions also applies to the propositions attributing goodness to other propositions. This suggests infinite chains of value propositions, so that it seems natural to suppose that only the bottom member of each chain need be measured in order to determine the values that accrue to the universe when a certain proposition is true. I have discussed elsewhere[13] some of the problems of measuring values. Here we need mention the principle:

GP.4. "It is good (It is good (*p))" is equivalent to "It is good (*p)."

---

12. See the second paper mentioned in footnote 8.
13. See the paper mentioned in footnote 3.

Consider then the following deduction, where 'It is good that' will be abbreviated to 'G', and the assumption is made that the goodness of propositions is the same as the goodness of intentions.

11.	$G(p \lor i) \leftrightarrow p \lor G(i)$	GI.2
12.	$G(G(p \lor i)) \leftrightarrow G(p \lor G(i))$	GPI.3
13.	$G(p \lor i) \leftrightarrow G(G(p)) \lor G(G(i))$	GP.4, GP.2
14.	$G(p \lor i) \leftrightarrow G(p) \lor G(i)$	GPI.4
15.	$p \lor G(i) \leftrightarrow G(p) \lor G(i)$	11, 14

Clearly, 15 is false. For a good state of affairs may be unrealized and some intentions are not good.

The immediate reply to that deduction is to reject the view that there are propositions that attribute goodness to propositions that themselves attribute goodness to another proposition or to an intention. Thus, step 12 is blocked. Can we, therefore, claim that the goodness of propositions is the same as the goodness of intentions? I don't think so. It seems to me that mixed conjunctive intentions abide by the following principle:

GI.5. "It is good of X (to A & p)" is equivalent to "p & it is good of X to A."

In GI.5 the symbol '&' of conjunction and the expression '(to A & p)' can be read in different ways, depending on the particular example. There are, however, two general readings which I find interesting: (i) 'to A while it is the case that p' and (ii) 'to A, it being the case that p'. It is noteworthy that whereas 'while' is often a genuine subordinating adverb of time (in the grammarians' terminology), 'while it is the case that' is an expression of mixed logical conjunction, and has nothing to do with time.

Whether or not the goodness of propositions is iterative, we must acknowledge this principle:

GP.6. "It is good that either it is good that q or p" is equivalent to "Either it is good that q or it is good that p."

Once again *assume* that the goodness of propositions is the same as the goodness of intentions; recall the previous abbreviations, and consider the following argument:

31.	$p \leftrightarrow (p \& G(i)) \lor p$	tautology
32.	$p \leftrightarrow G(p \& i) \lor p$	GI.5
33.	$G(p) \leftrightarrow G(G(p \& i) \lor p)$	GPI.3
34.	$G(p) \leftrightarrow G(p \& i) \lor G(p)$	GP.6
35.	$G(p) \leftrightarrow (p \& G(i)) \lor G(p)$	GI.5

Clearly, 35 is false in case p & $G(i)$ is true and $G(p)$ is false, as may very well happen.

This seems to me to demonstrate that the goodness of intentions is a different property from the goodness of propositions. The goodness ascribed to the mixed intention-proposition disjunction in (G.11) has nothing to do with the propositional component of that disjunction. The propositional component cannot be a focus or a subject of the goodness ascribed to the whole disjunction which is ascribable, of necessity, to each intentional component. Thus, if propositions cannot be focuses or subjects of the goodness of intentions, then the goodness they can be focuses of is different from the one ascribable to intentions.

IV. *Two Objections*

One premise of my argument in the preceding section has been attacked. It has been suggested that (G.11), "It will be good of Jones to do the following: to apologize to Smith by letter unless the mailmen go on a strike," and (G.11.a), "Unless the mailmen go on a strike, it will be good of Jones to apologize to Smith by letter," differ only in the order of their disjuncts, that in (G.11) the propositional disjunct "the mailmen go on a strike" is not within the scope of 'goodness', i.e., the operator "it will be good of Jones that." In other words, on this view, my punctuation of sentence (F.11) is incorrect; it should be 'It will be good of Jones to do the following: to apologize to Smith by letter; unless the mailmen go on a strike'.[14]

That won't do. There are propositions in which goodness is ascribed to a mixed compound intention, so that there *is* proposition (G.11) as I described it above. To nail this down, consider

(G.13)   It would be good of Jones to do the following: both to pick up Mary at the station if *she comes* and to talk to Myrna if *she calls.*

In this case the complex intention to which goodness is ascribed is a conjunction, and each conjunct is a conditional intention having a proposition, flagged by italicization, as antecedent. Obviously, the proposition "Mary comes" cannot be shown not to be in the scope of goodness by merely repunctuating the sentence (G.13). It might be suggested that sentence (G.13) is merely an abbreviation of the sentence

(G.14)   It would be good of Jones to pick up Mary at the station, if she comes; and it would also be good of Jones to talk to Myrna, if she calls.

14. This suggestion was made in class by both James Tomberlin and David MacCaskill sometime in 1967.

(G.13) is an abbreviation of (G.14), it may be said, in the same way in which (a) 'Jones and Mary are here' is an abbreviation of (b) 'Jones is here and Mary is here'. But this suggestion is amiss. Statement (G.14) may be true while (G.13) is false. In general, to speak crudely, from the fact that two intentions are each, individually, good, it does *not* follow that their conjunction is also good. And this is true whether the intentions in question are conditional or not.

Several friends[15] have suggested that I should consider the view that (G.13) is simply a stylistic variant of

> (G.15)   If Mary comes and Myrna calls, it will (would) be good of Jones both to pick up Mary and to talk with Myrna.

If this view were correct, then my reply to the objection falls to pieces, for the propositions "Mary comes" and "Myrna calls" are not really within the scope of the operator or property goodness. I, however, find that (G.13) and (G.15) are *not* equivalent. For one thing, if Mary comes and Myrna calls we cannot infer from (G.13) that it will (would) be good of Jones both to pick up Mary and to talk to Myrna. Yet in such a case this conclusion can be derived from (G.15) by a simple modus ponens.

A second objection to my argument in section III attempts to torpedo it by attacking its conclusion. It is this:[16] we can say in English without ungrammaticality:

> (G.16)   It was good of Jones to come and that we were still there when he arrived.

Patently, to the extent that one feels that (G.16) is grammatically correct one tends to feel that exactly the same concept, whether property or operator, is being expressed by the prefix 'It was good'. Yet, even though I would be happy to claim that (G.16) is ungrammatical, I do not intend to do so. I content myself with rejecting the premise that links the grammaticality of (G.16) with the semantical thesis that there is no ambiguity in the prefix 'It was good'. I want to maintain that 'It was good' is ambiguous between 'It was good of John' and 'It was good that.' It is intriguing that the ambiguity is a necessary part of the proper interpretation of the sentence. In short, I claim that (G.16) is an abbreviation in the surface grammar of

> (G.16a)   It was good of Jones to come and it was good that we were still there when he arrived.

15. Particularly Romane Clark and Paul Eisenberg.
16. I owe this objection to Rollin Workman.

And I contend that the locutions 'it was good of' and 'it was good that' express *different* goodnesses, the former of intentions, the latter of propositions.

V. *Conclusion*

I submit, then, that: (I) intentions and propositions are mutually irreducible entities; (II) the goodness of intentions is an altogether different property or operator from the goodness of propositions.

I will speak of *propositional or factual goodness* to refer to the goodness ascribable to propositions, and of *deontic, or actional goodness* to refer to the goodness ascribable to intentions. We may speak of *value properties* to refer to propositional goodness and to properties definable or explainable in terms of propositional or factual goodness. We may speak of *deontic properties* to refer to properties definable in terms of deontic goodness. I will speak of pure value properties (and pure deontic properties) to refer to the properties defined in terms of propositional goodness (or deontic goodness) and logical relations only.

I call intentional goodness *deontic* because the preceding argument shows that the goodness involved in our paradigm (G.1), "It was good of Jones to come," is of the same type as *rightness, oughtness* and *wrongness* which, on my long-standing view, are operators on practitions.[17] I have held that the *deontic properties,* so-called sometimes, *are operators on prescriptions that yield propositions.* It was a pleasant surprise to find that there is a goodness that is an operator on first-person prescriptions and yields propositions, and that there is another goodness that operates on propositions. Thus, one question that opens up is: What are the relations of actional goodness to the other members of the deontic family?

This question will be left for another occasion.

17. See the essays cited in footnotes 4 and 5 above. This crucial principle linking prescriptions (or mandates) to propositions has characterized my conception of deontic logic as nonstandard since 1952, when I prepared *On the Logic of Commands,* a master's essay presented to the Graduate Faculty of the University of Minnesota.

An Analysis of Faith

Robert L. Patterson
Duke University

That a word should change its meaning and, although retained in the language, should henceforth be employed in a very different, perhaps in an almost antithetical, sense is a type of occurrence familiar enough to all students of philology. Sometimes the influences which initiated such a change can fairly easily be detected. Thus we readily understand how the word *lent,* which in Old English means the *spring,* should now be applied to the period of traditional self-denial in which Christians of certain sects engage at that season of the year. In other cases, however, the change of meaning gives rise to considerable astonishment and has about it an atmosphere of mystery. For example, it seems strange that the word *with,* which in Old English means *against,* and which is still employed in that sense after such verbs as *fight, struggle,* and *strive,* and in such compounds as *withstand* and *withhold,* should in general usage function in the stead of the Old English *mid.* To those of us who experience a certain emotional satisfaction in using the same words which our fathers used, and in the same sense in which they used them, for millenia before us, even in some instances from a period antedating the dispersal of the Indo-European peoples, such alternatives of meaning are productive of a sentimental disquiet, even though we recognize that for the purpose of communication no harm has been done.

When, however, the meaning which the word originally bore is such as to arouse a strong emotional response, something in the nature of an emotional aura invests the word itself, and continues to invest it even though the meaning change. It acquires, as it were, a sacred character; and, in whatever sense we employ it, we feel impelled to justify our right to do so. It has become a linguistic inheritance of which we will not suffer ourselves to be deprived. In such a situation the discrimination of the various meanings which the word has acquired becomes imperative if we are to understand each other.

In this paper I intend to discuss the various meanings attaching to the word *faith.* It is a word of primary importance in theology, and of scarcely less importance in philosophy. And, whatever may be true of some philosophers, we may confidently affirm that no contemporary theologian would be prepared to dispense with it.

Faith for the Roman Catholic

Let us begin our investigation by considering its employment by Roman Catholic thinkers. Whether these be Thomists, Scotists, or Augustinians we may feel sure that they will concur in accepting the traditional definition of *faith* as "the assent of the intellect at the command of the will." Why does the will command? Because demonstration is impossible and certainty, therefore, unattainable. Could the truth of the article in question be demonstrated, the intellect would be constrained to assent by its own inherent nature. The intervention of volition is necessitated by the impotence of the intellect to reach a conclusion by the exercise of its native powers. Why, however, does the intellect obey? Because merit is acquired by firmness of adhesion in a case where doubt is possible. Thus the notion of merit is essential to the concept of faith; otherwise the latter would be deprived of its raison d'etre.

From this it might seem to follow that, the greater the possibility of doubt, the greater will be the merit thus acquired. And that such has sometimes been taken to be the state of affairs has been well brought out by De Joinville's story of the conversation between the master of theology and his bishop concerning transsubstantiation. But here St. Thomas interjects a warning, moved no doubt by the perception that the doctrine is in danger of being rapidly transformed into a reductio ad absurdum. We must not, he tells us, "believe lightly." And, as an illustration of what he means by believing lightly, he indicates faith on the part of Moslems. That a subscriber to the Athanasian Creed should bring such an accusation against those who are required merely to affirm that "there is no God but Allah, and Muhammad is the Apostle of Allah," can hardly fail at first glance to impress us as manifesting intellectual presumption of the most extreme type. We may become somewhat mollified, however, when we reflect that what Aquinas would seem to have in mind is the fact that Muhammad is not credited with the possession of miraculous powers. Thus St. Thomas boldly appeals to the miracles performed by Christ and the Apostles as grounds of faith.[1] It would appear, therefore, that faith must have something to build upon; that it is not merely a shot in the dark, as it were. There must be something suggestive of the claim advanced, yet insufficient of itself to establish the truth thereof. Hence

1. Aquinas appeals also to the heroism of the martyrs and the marvellous spread of Christianity, but here he is on more debatable *terrain,* for other religions have had their martyrs and their glorious ages of expansion.

it is clear that, without the conjunction of the concept of merit, the whole doctrine of faith would be rendered utterly pointless. Moreover faith is not left altogether defenseless. For, although an article of faith must be accepted upon authority, and although the content thereof may exceed the grasp of human reason, it will nevertheless always be possible, we are told, for human reason to refute any objections advanced by sceptics or unbelievers. In view of the nature of some of the articles of faith this is a bold claim; yet St. Thomas makes it, and perhaps he could hardly be expected to do less.

Our present concern being, not with the content of the articles, but with the act of faith itself, let us scrutinize the situation a little more closely. We have seen that the will is master, and that the intellect is obedient thereto. But how does the will know what commands to issue? It commands us to accept the teachings of the Church, we are informed. Certainly it does; but that it should do so is with equal certainty not a matter of chance, otherwise the will might with equal likelihood have ordered us to accept the doctrines of Islam or of Buddhism. In other words the will must be antecedently enlightened before it issues its commands. There must be a prior judgment with respect to the trustworthiness of the Church's teaching.

This reflection is reinforced by the consideration that the existence of God is emphatically declared by St. Thomas not to be an article of faith. It is a preamble to the articles, and it is so because, unlike the articles of faith, it is capable of being demonstrated. True enough the creed affirms "I believe in God," yet this belief is susceptible of being transformed into knowledge. Needless to say, not every Christian is able to prove the existence of God, but every Christian is presumed to know that it can be proved and that philosophers have proved it. Were it otherwise our faith would be vain. Of course not every man who is convinced of the divine existence is also convinced that the Church is illumined by his Spirit and is entitled to speak for him, yet the plausibility of this contention is vastly enhanced by the definite knowledge that God does exist.

This line of thought brings out a further point of considerable importance, namely, that faith has a twofold nature. On the one hand it involves belief in certain propositions propounded upon authority; on the other hand it is the expression of loyalty and devotion to a divine Sovereign. These two aspects of faith are found in conjunction everywhere in Christian experience, even in the earliest period. For Christianity is not a mere metaphysical system; it is an historic religion in the fullest sense of the word *historic*. It centers about the career and the mission of an historic figure. And faith has always been understood to involve both allegiance to Jesus as a person and acknowledgement of the validity of the claims made by him or for him. "Believe on the Lord Jesus Christ and thou shalt be saved" may be taken as a condensation of the message of the New Testament. Thus the two attitudes of devotion to a person and acceptance of propositions imposed by authority tend, so to speak, to suffuse each other. Hence heresy has always been excoriated, not merely as error, but also as treason.

This makes it easier for us to understand why the assent of the intellect should be regarded as meritorious. Yet it does not answer the further question, How does the intellect manage to accomplish such a feat? For the very notion of such an act is irreconcilable with its essential nature. The assent of the intellect is never fortuitous nor volitional; it assents when, and in so far, as it is constrained to do so by the evidence and the arguments presented to it. Let the will intervene, and the functioning of the intellect is thrown completely out of gear. Is it not clear, then, it may be asked, that faith is only another name for intellectual dishonesty and insincerity?

Is there anything that we can say to mitigate the acerbity of this attack? We may point out, in the first place, that the intellect often contemplates as probable assumptions upon which the will is prepared to act as though they were certain. Imagine, for example, a man lost in a forest. If he stay where he is, he will die of hunger and thirst. He does not know in which direction to walk, or he would not be lost. Yet his only chance of escape will be to move steadily in one direction, advancing in a straight line from tree to tree in order to keep from wandering in a circle. Let him, then, decide upon some direction which seems to offer more promise than any other, or, if there be no indications which offer any suggestions however faint, let him choose one direction at random and walk therein as determinedly as though he knew it to be the right one. Or take the case of a general who is about to engage in battle with a force approximately equal to his own. He believes that victory is possible, or he would seek to avoid the combat; yet he cannot regard it as certain. But, having once so decided, he must act as though it were certain, for, if doubt render his movements confused and wavering, defeat will be inevitable.

Let us take next the case of the Buddha who is reported to have exclaimed upon his attainment of deliverance, "the doors of immortality are open. Let those who would enter show faith." Faith is what? In Nirvāna? But why should they believe in what to them was incomprehensible, as the Buddha well realized that it was, since he always described it in negative terms? In his teaching? But what proof of it had he to offer? Was it not faith in him as being emphatically the kind of person that a deliverer from bondage might be expected to be? Here we have three cases of action in accord with unproved assumptions taken as true.

The situation becomes more complicated when we consider the attitude of the Thomist. Here we find doctrinal statements enough in all conscience. And, what makes the situation worse, some of these statements seem to have no intelligible meaning. Take, for instance, the assertion that there are three Persons in the Godhead. How can we rationalize this statement without falling either into tritheism or Sabellianism? St. Thomas assures us that we cannot comprehend it, so there is no use in our trying. Yet how can the intellect believe when it does not know what it believes? To believe what is unmeaning is surely like attempting to eat what is inedible. What actually happens, I think, is something like this. The "believer" makes the judgment, "While this proposition has no intelligible meaning for me, I can believe that this is due to the limitations of my intelligence and that it could be seen to be so by an intelligence superior to mine." Many of us make a somewhat similar judgment with respect to some of the assertions of the relativity people. It is in consequence of this judgment that the will acts in issuing its command, otherwise its action would be entirely sporadic and unaccountable. The assent of the intellect consists in its abstaining from offering any objection, and in allowing the will to act *as if* the incomprehensible proposition were true, that is, by investing it with an atmosphere of sacredness. In the spiritual realm this may be said to correspond to the decision of the intellect of the man lost in the forest to permit his will to determine the direction and the prosecution of his peregrination.

On the assumption that the preceding attempt to characterize fairly and accurately the Roman Catholic conception of faith has been successful what are we to say of it? It is not immediately evident that we need say anything further of it, inasmuch as our effort has been directed primarily at seeing it as it is, and to distinguishing it from other conceptions of faith. Yet there are one or two features of it to which it may be worth our while to direct our attention.

In the first place it might plausibly be assumed—and the philosopher, I presume, would be inclined to make such an assumption—that the purpose of revelation must be to communicate some intelligible teaching, and that a revelation which did not succeed in doing so would fail of its purpose. As a matter of fact some Christians have held this view, and to it we shall have hereafter to return. But such, as we have seen, is not the Thomist view. Revelation, thereafter, must serve some further purpose. And this purpose would seem to be the calling forth of an obedient and loyal response which is moral rather than intellectual. That the embracing of such a view might lead to the extravagances of a Sir Thomas Browne is its obvious danger; hence Aquinas's warning that we must not "believe lightly" is highly significant. Faith, it would seem, must be directed upon the probable. What the Deity desires is, not the immolation of the intellect, but rather the purification of the will. The line between "believing lightly" and believing meritoriously is a somewhat shadowy one, yet in theory at least it is always discernible. That the notion of the acquirement of merit should be involved in the very essence of faith is a proposition which has not been accepted by all Christians. We cannot do better, therefore, than at once to direct our attention to a point of view from which such an attitude is heartily and emphatically repudiated. Let us turn, accordingly, to Calvinism.

Faith for the Calvinist

The Thomist and the Calvinist are agreed that original sin is transmitted from generation to generation, that humanity as a whole is consequently infected thereby, and thereby alienated from God, and that the impartation of grace is essential for salvation. It was this doctrine which was passionately denounced by the nineteenth century liberal; and I, for one, have no inclination to quarrel with his verdict. Indeed, I should venture to affirm that the condemnation of Pelagius inflicted upon orthodox Christianity an injury from which it has never recovered. But what the nineteenth century liberal and I think of the matter is not now to the point. Between the Thomist and the Calvinist one finds, however, an important divergence of opinion in that the former, in opposition to the latter, holds to the reality of free will, although he asserts that the concurrence of divine grace is essential to its exercise. This clearly is, to say the least, a "subtle doctrine." An act of will, St. Thomas tells, is necessary if it be entailed by previous volitions and antecedent circumstances, and it is free if it be not thus entailed. Yet this necessity and freedom are relative only to previous events in the temporal process. Since God is the ultimate cause of all events, every act is dependent upon him. A man wills necessarily if God wills that he so will, and freely if God so wills. In the light of these declarations it may be questioned whether the Calvinist does more than state with brutal frankness what the Thomist ought to admit if he were logical. But the important point for our present consideration is that, together with free will, the Calvinist rejects in toto the notion of merit, and thereby frees the conception of faith from any connection therewith.

We must next take cognizance of an equally important point of difference. For the Thomist, as we have observed, the existence of God can be demonstrated. The divine existence, therefore, is not an article of faith, but only a preamble to the articles; and it is this knowledge that God does exist which is the ultimate ground and justification of faith. This contention the Calvinist energetically repudiates. God, he affirms, cannot be reached, nor his existence demonstrated, by human reason. Before God, accordingly, man stands both morally and intellectually stripped. Neither action nor thought on his part is of any avail. Salvation is from God alone. Well has the Calvinist chosen his motto, *Soli Deo Gloria!*

How does this salvation come about? We must recognize, in the first place, that man despite his own natural incapacity, has not as a matter of fact, been left totally devoid of all knowledge of God. What by the exercise of his own native powers he cannot attain to has been freely bestowed upon him. For there is a common grace, imparted by God to all normal human beings, which implants in them an awareness of the divine. This bestowal of common grace does not suffice to insure man's salvation; on the contrary, it merely leaves him "without excuse" – or, to put it bluntly, justifies his damnation. It does not appear, therefore, that man has any reason to evince gratitude for the gift. There is, however, a special grace vouchsafed to those individuals who are predestined to salvation. It is the *testimonium Spiritus Sancti internum* which resounds throughout Reformed theology like the sound of a trumpet. It is this which fills the dogmatic body of Calvinism with the dynamic pulsation of mystical life. It is this with which every Christian, so Calvin tells us, is experientially aware; it is this which enables him to recognize that the Bible is the word of God with the same assurance as that with which he recognizes that sugar is sweet. The same Spirit, Calvin affirms, which spoke through the prophets and apostles and gave us the external revelation embodied in the Scriptures bears witness in our souls to the divine source of the revelation thereby conveyed to us, and thus authenticates to us its message. And it is this conjunction of an outer and an inner revelation which protects us against the excesses of such extremists as the Sqickau Prophets and the Anabaptists who profess to expound an "unwritten word" which is not contained in the Scriptures, thus depriving the latter of their proper authority.

For a development of this conception of faith we may resort to the writings of Jonathan Edwards, not that we may hope to discover in it any view which contradicts Calvin's teaching but rather to find there an aspect of Calvin's thought brought into the center of attention and given forceful expression. In developing his position Edwards makes use of the third type of idea of which Locke speaks; an idea, namely, which is derived neither from sensation nor from reflection but which Locke identifies with "that first impression which is made immediately by God in the mind of any man, to which we cannot set any bounds."[2] This idea, Edwards goes on to assure us, is "different from all that can be in the minds of natural men"; it is a "sense of the heart," a "sense of the beauty of holiness." This development is of great importance, for it makes the experience of divine grace essentially aesthetic in character; and Edwards is quite within his rights when he likens it to an appreciation of noble music

2. *Essay,* bk. IV. cap. XVIII, sec. 3.

or of high courtesy. And the impartation of it is like "opening the blind eyes, raising the dead, and bringing a person into a new world." From this it follows that the recipients of special grace are raised to a supernatural level while still in this life, so that in a sense which is more than mere metaphor we may venture to say with Sir Thomas Browne that "the glory of the world is surely over and the earth is already in ashes unto them."

Viewed from this angle Calvinism becomes transformed into a religion of intellectual or spiritual beauty. Is this the reason, we may ask, why the typical Calvinistic church is so simple in structure, so devoid of ornamentation, why it consists in Froude's words of "four bare white walls which seem to say that no lies are to be spoken or acted between them"? Calvin does, indeed, teach that the function of the artist is to show forth the glory of God, yet it would seem that he held that in religion we have so completely transcended the physical and sensible that the manifestation of God's glory must be in the human soul.

A man must surely be blind to spiritual beauty who finds nothing impressive in the thought of Calvin, especially as reinterpreted by Edwards. Now we understand, we might exclaim, why the Calvinist refuses to enter upon the toilsome path of argumentation. Has he not shown us "a more excellent way"? What are arguments to him who has seen the heavens open? Moreover this noble insight is bound by no logical connection to the inherited doctrines of original sin, election, predestination, and everlasting damnation, and can without difficulty be separated from them. Furthermore what it affirms with respect to the Judaec Christian Scriptures and their function of manifesting the divine beauty can, without involving us in any contradiction, be affirmed with respect to much of the sacred literature of other religions. We who can read, as Calvin and Edwards could not read, the Upanisads and the poetry of the Sufis may well feel that an open door has been set before us that no man can shut. A philosophy of religion based upon religious experience, and upon religious experience alone, seems to be unfolding itself before us; and the spectacle may well evoke in us a mood of exultation.

Let us, however, turn our attention for the moment to the fundamental disagreement between the Calvinist and the Thomist, the nature of which now becomes clear to us. Nothing is more impressive than the unanimity with which Thomistic writers put aside as inconclusive the *argumentum ex experientia religiosa*. We cannot, they affirm, rely upon an experience, however appealing, which is uncriticized and unevaluated, without the risk of falling into error; and we can properly criticize and evaluate it only in the light of an independently acquired metaphysical position. Hence we cannot rationally hope to dispense with the intellectual task of following the "five ways" of St. Thomas. The preamble to the articles of faith must be made good by arguments based ultimately upon sense-experience, and for these religious experience provides no substitute. From this contention the Calvinist dissents with equal vehemence. No argument, he may point out, has ever convinced everybody; whereas the witness of the Spirit, he maintains, carries with it complete and infallible assurance.

Now there is a question which we can ask the Calvinist and which he ought to be able to answer in the affirmative if the impressiveness of his position is not to be seriously diminished. As we have seen, faith, for him, is intuitive insight. And, if it be completely self-sufficient, it should carry him the whole way. But this means that it involves direct apprehension of its object. Can the Calvinist, however, cite in his own defense and apply to himself the words of the Gospel, "Blessed are the pure in heart for they shall see God"? If he claims less than this, can we not accuse him of evading the issue? Yet is it not quite clear that he cannot make this claim? For Calvin has taught that we cannot know God as he is in himself, but only as he appears to us. This is a concession which might mean much or little. Let us, therefore, for the moment disregard it and turn to Edwards, from whom we receive a frank reply. From the revelation of divine beauty in the Scriptures and in nature to the divine Revealer there is, he tells us, but "one step," and the inference is "immediate." But there is a step, and there is an inference; therefore, as he honestly admits, there is an argument.[3] This is obviously the *argumentum ex experientia religiosa.* It may be a better argument than the Thomist thinks it is. But it is an argument all the same. The Thomist camel, therefore, has its nose under the Calvinistic tent. Though faith be insight yet it requires to be supplemented by reason, and this is a serious admission for the Calvinist to make.

I have called attention to this aspect of the situation because there is conceivably something more that might be said, although the Calvinist has not said it. The current of Augustinianism with its doctrine of illumination divided at the beginning of the modern era into two streams. One of these is Calvinism, and the course of its current carries us at once beyond the boundaries of Roman Catholicism. The other current, which flowed within these boundaries, was that of Ontologism. And what the Ontologist had to say should be of interest to the student of Calvinism.

The Position of the Ontologists

We must not turn to Ontologism in the expectation of encountering a new definition of faith, for the Ontologists were Roman Catholics and

3. *A Treatise Concerning Religious Affections,* pt. III, sec. 5.

were content to accept the traditional definition. The reason why I shall briefly discuss their point of view is that, despite the difference of terminology, they were as concerned with intuitive insight as is the Calvinist, and they believed it possible to avoid the predicament in which the Calvinist seems to have involved himself.

The first point of difference which we shall notice turns out not to be as significant as it appears to be at first sight, and is related to such knowledge of God as is possessed by all men. Since they hold such knowledge to be above the capacity of human nature, Calvinists, as we have seen, attribute it to common grace. For the Ontologists, on the contrary, it is a natural knowledge with which all human beings are endowed at their creation. Yet what is this but a "distinction without a difference"? A common grace which is so common that all men partake of it – how is it to be distinguished from man's natural capacity for the possession of which he is likewise indebted to the Deity? The disagreement would appear to be purely verbal, and I think that we may venture to disregard it.

The Ontologist, however, has something further to add which is of interest. The knowledge of God which is common to all men, he tells us, is both direct and confused. The confusion accounts for the fact that the directness is often lost sight of. Yet, if such knowledge be direct, man, whether he realize it or not, is actually in contact with God.

Having said so much the Ontologist must now reply to a formidible and twofold argument advanced against him by his coreligionists of the Thomistic tradition. Direct knowledge of God, it is urged, can be nothing else than intuition of the divine Essence. But, if this be conceded, two impossible consequences follow. In the first place all men will be *in patria,* for Heaven is nothing other than the *visio Dei.* And, in the second place, since God is a triune God, the three Persons of the Trinity will be intuited. But it is undeniably the case that not all men are in Heaven, and that not all men are directly aware of God's triune nature.

To defend himself against this attack the Ontologist proceeded to draw a "distinction of reason" between the *"essence intime,"* which is the divine nature as it is in itself, and the *"essence extime"* which is the divine nature as apprehended by human beings, and conformably thereto between two types of direct awareness – *intuition,* which is awareness of the *essence intime,* and which is enjoyed by the saints *in patria,* and *extuition,* an awareness which is possessed by men on earth.[4] What is "extuited" is the infinity of God, and such awareness does not attain to a stage of intimacy wherein the Trinity itself can be directly cognized.

Ingenuous as this defense may be, it might seem illegitimate to distinguish between two modes of direct apprehension, especially when our

4. These distinctions are elaborated and defended by Jules Fabre d'Envieu in his two treatises entitled *Defense de L'Ontologisme* and *Response aux Lettres d'un Sensualiste.*

concern is with the apprehension of God. For, according to the Scholastics and Neoscholastics, there is no distinction in God between substance and attribute or between attribute and attribute; there is only an absolute, yet fecund, simplicity. Nevertheless, the Ontologist was able triumphantly to point to St. Thomas's express statement to the effect that the vision of God vouchsafed to one soul *in patria* may be superior to that granted to another. How there could conceivably be these degrees of apprehension of a purely simple Being we need not inquire. What I wish to point out is that the Ontologist's distinction between the *essence intime* and the *essence extime* would seem reminiscent of Calvin's distinction between God as he is in himself and God as he appears to us. It may be, then, that we have been unjust to Calvin in allowing Edwards to interpret him to us; it may be that Edwards's "one step" and "immediate" inference are out of place, and that Calvin and the Ontologists are at one in holding that the divine Essence is somehow directly apprehended although not as it is in itself. However this may be we shall agree, I think, that, while there is a difference between an experience and the interpretation of that experience, this is not the same as the difference between what is experienced and what is not experienced but only inferred. Calvin's contention that faith is intuitive insight is plainly vastly more impressive if Edwards's inference be omitted.

Another point of interest is the Ontologist's assertion that man's natural awareness of God is, not only direct, but also confused. For in the elimination of such confusion argument would surely be in place, not to take us beyond the evidence but to clarify, explicate, and reinforce the evidence. Hence the Calvinistic repudiation of all argument would seem to be indicative of an extreme attitude, and Edwards's resort to the *argumentum ex experientia religiosa* could, in this perspective, be hailed as a step in the right direction.

Lockian Faith

So much stress has been laid upon the empiricism of Locke that attention has been in great measure directed away from his discussion of the relationship between reason and faith, and this despite the fact that it was this aspect of his teaching which most profoundly impressed his contemporaries, and which in the following centuries exerted so powerful an influence upon the Unitarians of New England. And it is well worth considering with care, not only because of its wide influence but also because of its own merits.

Locke's conception of faith, we shall find, is very different from the Calvinist's, and to some extent more nearly resembles that of the Roman

Catholic, even as his view of the function of reason may be said to be more closely allied to that of St. Thomas than to that of Calvin. None the less his opinion with regard to each of these topics is his own, and was to a considerable extent revolutionary. We must bear in mind that in his religious thinking Locke was a pioneer whose effort was directed toward the development of Protestantism beyond the limits of traditional orthodoxy. He was above all things a devoted rationalist, yet rationalism did not mean for him what it meant for some of the deists. Far from involving a rejection of the claims of revelation, it substantiated them. The twin concepts of revelation and of faith were in Locke's eyes rational through and through, and the man who rejected them was not a genuine rationalist. Whereas, unlike Calvin, he did not disparage reason, unlike St. Thomas he did not attempt to bring reason and faith into a somewhat awkward alliance of mutually sovereign powers. His solution was to subordinate faith to reason, yet this very subordination was to render faith absolutely invulnerable.

Locke begins his discussion of faith by describing it as assent to revelation. This sounds exceedingly Thomistic, nor is this initial impression removed when Locke goes on to assure us that faith "as absolutely determines our minds, and as perfectly excludes all wavering as our knowledge itself; and we may as well doubt of our own being, as we can, whether any revelation from God be true. So that faith is a settled and pure principle of assent and assurance, and leaves no manner of room for doubt or hesitation."[5] It is true that Locke at once proceeds to qualify his assertion by announcing that the degree of assent depends upon the character of the evidence, so that, if the evidence provide only an apparent probability, the degree of assent will correspond thereto; yet even this admission does not seem wholly incompatible with St. Thomas's warning that we must not "believe lightly."

Our initial impression may indeed be strengthened when we reflect that Locke completely agrees with St. Thomas in his view that the existence of God can be demonstrated; in fact he goes so far as to declare that the evidence is "equal (If I mistake not) to mathematical certainty."[6] Obviously Aquinas himself could ask for no more. The proof upon which Locke relies is the *argumentum ex contingentia mundi,* known also in post-Kantian times as the cosmological argument; and Locke states it very forcibly, and develops it with great thoroughness.

The ultimate divergence between the views of the two thinkers is first suggested by Locke's protest against opposing reason to faith, which he declares to "be in itself a very improper way of speaking, yet common

5. *Essay,* bk. IV, cap. XVI, sec. 14.
6. Ibid., bk. IV, cap. X, sec. I.

use has so authorized it, that it would be folly either to oppose or hope to remedy it";[7] and accordingly he announces that he will himself proceed in conformity with it. Before doing so, however, he enters the following caveat: "I think it may not be amiss to take notice, that however faith be opposed to reason, faith is nothing but a firm assent of the mind; which, if it be regulated as is our duty, cannot be afforded to anything but upon a good reason, and so cannot be opposite to it. He that believes without having any reason for believing, may be in love with his own fancies, but neither seeks truth as he ought, nor pays the obedience due to his Maker, who would have him use those discerning faculties he has given him."[8]

Faith, then, is grounded upon reason. But what of the man who "believes without any reason for believing"? Is such a state psychologically possible? If Locke's previous statement be true, is not such a faith a contradiction in terms? Rational assent clearly differs from irrational assent; hence, if both be called by the same name, it must surely be because the will is operative in both. Yet how can the will operate in rational assent, which, as Locke has told us, should be constrained by the evidence before it? There may be some confusion here; yet I think that we shall not be far wrong if we conclude that Locke's view is that the will, if it does its duty, can constrain the mind to consider fairly and impartially the evidence presented, but that, if it does not perform its duty and suffers itself to be perverted, the will may permit the mind to be overwhelmed by the clamors of "enthusiasm." "Enthusiasm" in religion is Locke's great bugbear, and doubtless, having been an observer of the extravagances of the Commonwealth period, he knew what he was talking about.

Let us now turn, however, to the well-known passage in which, in accordance with his previously declared resolution, Locke proceeds to "contradistinguish" reason and faith. "Reason," he writes, "I take to be the discovery of the certainty or probability of such propositions or truths, which the mind arrives at by deduction made from such ideas which it has got by the use of its natural faculties, viz. by sensation or reflection.

"Faith, on the other side, is the assent to any proposition not thus made out by the deductions of reason, but upon the credit of the proposer, as coming from God, in some extraordinary way of communication. This way of discovering truths to man we call revelation."[9]

In connection with the above definition of faith there are two points which attract our attention. The first is that Locke makes no distinction between the faith which is a belief without reasons for believing and the faith which is a degree of assent based upon the nature of the evidence before it. We may suspect, rightly I think, that the definition is framed to

7. Ibid., bk. IV, cap. XVII, sec. 24.
8. Loc. cit.
9. Ibid., bk. IV, cap. XVIII, sec. 2.

cover both kinds of faith but that Locke's interest is now directed upon the latter. In the second place we notice that the propositions to which faith assents cannot "be made out by the deductions of reason." In the case of propositions the truth of which we can demonstrate for ourselves the intervention of revelation would be pointless, since it could never offer us an assurance equal to that which we acquire through the observation of the agreement or disagreement of our ideas. It is true that we can become certain that God exists, and from it follows that any revelation which he has imparted is certainly true; but this does not settle the question whether any particular instance of what purports to be revelation *is* revelation.

It is where reason fails to demonstrate that revelation comes to our aid. And Locke has chosen two very good examples of the kind of propositions which he takes to be the content of revelation. How could we conceivably know, he asks us, by any process of ratiocination that there had been war in Heaven, or that the bodies of the dead will be raised at the Last Day? Plainly such knowledge can be derived only from revelation. But now the question arises, How are we to determine whether what purports to be revelation is revelation? Of the possibility of revelation we are fully assured, inasmuch as we are certain that God exists; what concerns us is its actuality.

Here is where Locke is at the furthest remove from Calvinism, and also from St. Thomas. The notion that the validity of objective revelation contained in the Scriptures is authenticated by any subjective experience of intuitive insight directly imparted by the Holy Spirit Locke brushes aside. How can we evaluate such an experience? In this region any fool can make any claims, and such claims can neither be confirmed nor refuted. Nor is there any merit to be acquired by assenting to what we cannot understand, not that Locke is opposed to the notion of merit. No ethical thinker ever emphasized with more blatant frankness that the great motive for good conduct is the hope of divine reward and the fear of divine punishment. But, when it comes to believing, the merit consists in forming as sound a judgment as we can upon the basis of the evidence presented. God is a rational Being, and he desires us to be as rational as possible.

From this it follows that, if God sent us a messenger to proclaim revealed truth, he will provide that messenger with unmistakable credentials. And these credentials must be open to the inspection of all men; hence we must look for them in the common world of sense-experience.

Here we come to Locke's famous doctrine of miracles which has often been so severely criticized, and which I shall not undertake to discuss in detail. It is, in my opinion, more respectable than it is frequently made out to be. It has often been said that Locke holds that physical occurrences can authenticate spiritual teachings, and that this is nonsense. But what miracles directly authenticate is, not the teaching set forth, but the status of the teacher or prophet. The teaching itself must be such as to fulfill various requirements. It must be worthy of its divine origin, bearing upon fundamental concerns. It must be intelligible and devoid of self-contradiction. And it must be in harmony with all antecedently communicated revelations similarly vindicated.

We must remember that, when Locke wrote, the four Gospels were generally believed to have been written by the men to whom they are ascribed, and to contain the unimpeachable testimony of eye-witnesses. Today, of course, the whole situation is changed. While any thinker who believes in a creative God is logically compelled to acknowledge the possibility of miraculous occurrences, it is a very different thing to assert that they actually did occur. How far any accounts in the Gospels approximate to firsthand testimony is a matter of conjecture, and the study of comparative religion has familiarized us with the ease with which a belief in miracles can arise.

With regard to Locke we must also observe that for him there is no question of believing in "mysteries." Despite his unwillingness openly to avow his Socinianism, there can be little doubt that he did not accept the Doctrines of the Trinity and the Incarnation. In his view we are required only to believe in the existence of God, the Messiahship of Jesus, and the Last Judgment; and, whether or not these doctrines be true, they are surely intelligible.

What Locke has given us, then, is a rationalism which substantiates and includes supernaturalism. Faith is rational assent to intelligible propositions satisfactorily authenticated. Christianity is thus rational throughout.

It will be of some interest to consider the effect of Locke's influence, after the lapse of more than a century, upon an American thinker who was the most eminent among the founders of the Unitarian movement yet who was by no means a thorough-going disciple, namely, William Ellery Channing. In the first place we notice that the term *faith* is used by Channing in a broader sense than that of mere intellectual assent, for it embraces also the moral and emotional attitudes.

"Mere acts of the understanding," writes Channing, "are neither right nor wrong. When I speak of faith as a holy or virtuous principle, I extend the term beyond its primitive meaning, and include in it not merely the assent of the intellect, but the disposition and temper by which this assent is determined, and which it is suited to confirm; and I attach as broad a significance to unbelief, when I pronounce it a crime. The truth is, that the human mind, though divided by our philosophy into many distinct capacities, seldom or never exerts them separately, but generally blends them in one act. Thus, in forming a judgment, it exerts the will and affections, or the moral principles, of our nature, as well as the power of thought. Men's passions and interests mix with, and are expressed in, the decisions of the intellect. In the Scriptures, which use language freely, and not with philosophical strictness, faith and unbelief are mental acts of this complex character, or joint products of the understanding and heart; and on this account they are objects of approbation and reproof. In these views," he continues somewhat naively, "I presume, reflecting Christians of every name agree."[10]

I have cited *in extenso* Channing's description of faith because of its own inherent interest, for it clearly anticipates the outlook of the twentieth century critics of the "faculty psychology." His use of the term obviously has something in common both with that of the Roman Catholic and of the Calvinist. I doubt, however, whether his divergence from Locke be more than terminological, for Locke definitely distinguishes between the misguided faith of the "enthusiast" and the normal assent of the intellect in accordance with the evidence presented. That Channing and Locke are fundamentally at one is clear from the ringing tones, which Locke surely would have rejoiced to hear, in which Channing declares:

> Christianity is a rational religion. Were it not so, I should be ashamed to profess it. I am aware that it is the fashion with some to deny reason, and to set up revelation as an opposite authority. This error, though countenanced by good men, and honestly maintained for the defense of the Christian cause, ought to be earnestly withstood; for it virtually surrenders our religion into the hands of the unbeliever. It saps the foundation to strengthen the building. It places our religion in hostility to human nature, and gives its adversaries the credit of vindicating the rights and noblest powers of the mind.
>
> We must never forget that our rational nature is the greatest gift of God. For this we owe him our chief gratitude. It is a greater gift than any outward aid or benefaction, and no doctrine which degrades it can come from its Author. The development of it is the end of our being. Revelation is but a means, and is designed to concur with nature, providence, and God's spirit, in carrying forward reason to its perfection. I glory in Christianity because it enlarges, invigorates, exalts my rational nature. If I could not be a Christian without ceasing to be rational, I should not hesitate as to my choice. I feel myself bound to sacrifice to Christianity property,

10. *Works,* p. 190, col. I.

reputation, life; but I ought not to sacrifice to any religion that reason which lifts me above the brute and constitutes me a man.[11]

In conformity with this rationalistic outlook which he shares with Locke, and with his conception of faith, Channing flatly affirms that it is psychologically impossible to believe a mystery.[12] For the mysterious is something unknown, and concerning the unknown nothing can be believed. For belief must have content, whereas assent to a mystery would be equivalent to assent to nothing at all. Hence comes the great advantage of Unitarianism, for "an infinite Father is the most exalted of all conceptions, and yet the least perplexing."[13]

In concluding this brief survey we may note that Channing's most significant difference from Locke is with respect to intuitive knowledge, and that here his attitude closely approximates to that of the Calvinist or the Ontologist. "The highest truths," he declares, "are not those which we learn from abroad. No outward teaching can bestow them. They are unfolded from within, by our very progress in the religious life. New ideas of perfection, new convictions of immortality, a new consciousness of God, a new perception of our spiritual nature, come to us as revelations, and open upon us with a splendor which belongs not to this world."[14] Whether or not Channing would have included experiences such as these under the heading of faith is, perhaps, doubtful, although I think it likely that he would have done so. The point is of interest for our present inquiry, although in itself only of terminological importance. It is probable that we detect here the influence of the Platonic tradition so potent in early New England, and even more likely the influence of Price.

The line of development which we have just been tracing is one of great importance for the history of theology and of the philosophy of religion. Hegelianism is not the only source of rationalism. In Locke we see it at once validating and appropriating to itself the function of revelation; in Channing it proceeds to do the same with mysticism. The whole process is one of considerable magnificence. In this day of two-fold reaction, toward neoorthodoxy on the one hand, and toward linguistic analysis on the other, the strength of rationalism has been seriously underestimated. Yet increasing evidence of a desire on the part of the proponents of each point of view to enter into some sort of alliance is indicative of their unacknowledged awareness of where the real danger

11. Ibid., p. 233.
12. Ibid., p. 339; cf. James Freeman Clarke's succinct statement, "Where mystery begins in religion faith ends, and it ends just at that point."
13. *Works,* p. 389, col. II.
14. Ibid., p. 992, col. I.

lies, and of the enemy most to be dreaded. A reviving rationalism is likely once again to sweep the field.

Faith in Contemporary Thought

We have now before us three, or rather four, meanings which have been accorded to the word *faith* in the field of religion: (1) trust in and loyalty to a divine Person; (2) the assent of the intellect at the command of the will; (3) intuitive insight; and (4) the assent of the intellect to revealed truth to a degree corresponding to the weight of the evidence.

In contemporary Protestant thought we find no one usage generally agreed upon, and accordingly must inquire of each writer what his meaning is. Yet I believe that it is fair to say that the splendor of the Calvinistic *testimonium Spiritus Sancti internum* has been appreciably dimmed. On the whole we find subjective assurance emphasized rather than intuitive insight. Sometimes this assurance appears to be regarded as absolute; at others, when the influence of existentialism makes itself felt, we are told that the important thing is to decide, and to run the risks of our decision, risks which we have no right to seek to escape. In all this there seems to be a covert stress laid upon volition, upon "the assent of the intellect at the command of the will"; especially so when the existentialist influence is predominant. Despite the repudiation of the notion of merit, there is a certain approximation to the scholastic outlook.

While an almost hysterical emphasis is thus laid upon faith, there is a lack of general agreement as to whom or what we are to have faith in. Sometimes it is the "Jesus of history"; sometimes it is the "Christ of faith" who is frequently dissociated from the man Jesus to a degree which smacks of docetism. But, however faith is conceived, and whatever be its object, there is general agreement upon its vital importance; so that it almost seems that it is the word, rather than the meaning, that is of fundamental significance.

I now wish to call attention to yet another concept of faith, this time not to one advanced by a Christian theist but one put forward by an idealist. In his book entitled *Some Dogmas of Religion*, after pointing out that the moral quality of courage is requisite in the seeker for truth, McTaggart continues:

> And he will also need — unless he is almost incredibly fortunate — a certain form of faith. He will need the power to trust the conclusions which his reason has deliberately adopted, even when circumstances make such a belief especially difficult or painful. There are leaden days when even the most convinced idealist seems to *feel* that his

body and his furniture are as real as himself, and members of a far more powerful reality. There are times when the denial of immortality seems, to the most confirmed disbeliever in immortality, a denial which he has scarcely strength to make.

But, whatever is true, it is quite certain that truth is not affected by incidents like these. If all reality has been proved to be spiritual, it cannot have ceased to be spiritual because today I am ill or overworked. If I had no reason to believe in immortality yesterday, when other people's friends were dead, I have no greater reason to believe in it today because my friend has died.

If we want to know the truth, then, we must have faith in the conclusions of our reason, even when they seem—as they often will seem—too good or too bad to be true. Such faith has better claim to abide with hope and love than the faith which consists in believing without reasons for belief. It is this faith, surely, which is sought in the prayer, "Suffer us not for any pains of death to fall from thee". And for those who do not pray there remains the resolve that, so far as their strength may prevail, neither the pains of death nor the pains of life shall drive them to any comfort in that which they hold to be false, or drive them from any comfort in that which they hold to be true.

In this noble passage we discover a conception of faith which is other than those which we have previously considered. The trust advocated is not trust in a person, human or divine, but trust in reason. And this does not mean reliance upon our own individual capacities; it does not mean arrogating to ourselves infallibility. We find that there are able thinkers who differ from us, but this in itself proves neither that they are wrong nor that they are right. We are certainly prone to make mistakes, and it is our business to try to discover and to correct such mistakes. What McTaggart deprecates is what might be termed a "blanket doubt" which is grounded upon nothing in particular but extends over the entire range of our thinking, and embraces all our premises, inferences, and conclusions. Such doubt is at once irrational and enervating, and is productive of nothing but a state of irresolution. Such doubt cannot be removed by argument, for it is directed impartially upon all processes of argumentation. It can be dispelled only by a decision to rely upon reason. We have, then, a fifth definition of faith—trust in reason. It is a volitional attitude, yet one not adopted for the sake of acquiring merit, and, plainly, it is a concomitant of the Lockian positive assent in accordance with the evidence.

With all these definitions of faith before us, what are we to say of them? What I should say is that, inasmuch as the word has been used to cover such a variety of meanings, only intellectual confusions can result from continuing to employ it, and that in the interest of clarity it would be best to give it up altogether. It would surely be better to utilize a number of different words to signify these different meanings.

Take, for instance, the case dear to the pragmatist where immediate action is imperative yet evidence indicative of the course which we ought to adopt is either absent or conflicting to a degree which renders even a probable judgment impossible. The illustration of the man lost in the forest is appropriate. To abstain from acting at all would be fatal; *some* action continuously and consistently exerted is absolutely necessary. The choice of direction is unavoidably arbitrary, but, once made, must be persisted in as resolutely as though based upon certain information. Inasmuch as the choice is wholly dependent upon volition, the appropriate word in such a case is surely *decision*.

If, however, there be sufficient ground to form a judgment which, although highly uncertain, is yet in some degree probable, while equal firmness of determination is essential if the action is to be carried to a successful conclusion, volition will blend with some degree of hope and confidence. *Conviction* would seem to be the word which best indicates this complex psychological state.

What now shall we say of the scholastic "assent of the intellect at the command of the will"? I think that we must concede that Channing is right in his contention that it is psychologically impossible to believe a mystery, for the intellect can assent only to what it understands. Yet we can refuse to consult it, and can turn away our attention from it. In this sense alone can the will command. But I believe that I have shown that such volition must follow from an antecedent acceptance as probable of the judgment that the proposition to which assent is required, while unintelligible *quoad nos,* may yet have a meaning in itself which may be understood by an intelligence of a higher order than ours. If it be represented to us that such submission is essential to salvation, and that refusal on our part will result in everlasting damnation, the recognition of a very low degree of probability may suffice to produce a submissive attitude. Pascal's wager here comes to mind, and I fear that much Christian faith has been the product of the threat of hell fire.

When we turn to the direct apprehension of the Calvinist and the Ontologist we ought, probably, to make a further distinction. For the Calvinist such awareness is imparted by divine grace; accordingly we may appropriately term it *illumination*. Since for the Ontologist it is the exertion of a capacity inherent in human nature, the term *intuition* would seem suitable were it not for his distinction between awareness attainable in this life and that possessed by the saints *in patria,* in view of which it will perhaps be better to employ his own term *extuition*.

In so far as by *faith* we mean confidence in and loyalty to a divine

Person, because of the wisdom and goodness which the Deity is held to possess, it will surely be well to make use of the word which we habitually apply to a similar confidence reposed in a human person, wise and good, namely, *trust*.

As for the Lockian assent to revealed truth to a degree corresponding to the evidence presented, how can we do better than avail ourselves of the phrase which his description has made familiar, and call it *rational assent*. And of this the volitional obverse is plainly McTaggart's decision to rely steadfastly upon reason, an attitude which is clearly opposed to one of neurotic disquietude. For this I venture to propose the phrase *rational assurance*.

Whether the terms which I have ventured to suggest are the most satisfactory is obviously disputable. Yet I do believe that the result of the analysis herein presented does show that a terminological clarification of the situation is highly desirable. As we survey the theological world the unanimity with which faith is presented as absolutely essential together with the difference of opinion as to what it consists in and what it is directed upon does seem quite appalling. Certitude is a good thing, probability is good when better cannot be had, decision may be good or bad but is sometimes inescapably necessary. Yet why this constant caterwauling about faith? The very word has become sacrosanct, yet what it stands for is an intellectual, emotional, and volitional swamp where distinctions become blended in a sort of miasma. I do not presume to suppose, any more than did Locke, that my individual protest will avail to remedy the situation, yet, when the need for a protest is so imperative, one may feel impelled to make it, come what may.

Discrimination as an Example of
Moral Irrationality

Evan Simpson
McMaster University

In spite of its familiarity discrimination against other persons cannot be considered a normal phenomenon, and even persons charged with it consider such behavior aberrant. That they may intelligibly do so is evident from the nature of the concept. As the term is to be used here, discrimination is differential treatment with insufficient reason, and one may consider oneself to have good reasons for an action even if they are not apparent to a critic. Although discrimination is universally condemned, therefore, persons may disagree whether certain behavior is properly to be characterized as justifiably differential or whether it simply masquerades under the guise of reason. It is of considerable philosophical and social interest to be able to identify those reasons which make differential treatment legitimate, those which may make it excusable though discriminatory, and those which make it unequivocally blameworthy. What distinguishes these various sorts of reasons or purported reasons is (certain complications aside) that the first are founded upon true beliefs, the second upon false beliefs, and the third upon beliefs which are necessarily false. It can be shown, in other words, that those acts of discrimination which evoke moral condemnation coincide with a certain kind of irrational behavior—behavior based upon beliefs which one knows to be false, beliefs contradicted by others necessarily held by any rational person.

Discrimination belongs to a family of behavior ordinarily originating in and indicative of disrespect for certain types of person, and the present discussion concerns only an example of these related forms of behavior. Disrespect likewise has many features in common with other attitudes and emotions and some of these figure importantly in the analysis of discrimination. These features include three items of first importance. (1) Attitudes and emotions are conceptually tied to evaluations—not contingently and not by definition, but in a way which places their analysis within what is appropriately called the metaphysics of value. For this reason the main discussion is prefaced by a description of a contemporary version of this obsolete notion. (2) Each attitude and emotion has a characteristic cognitive content which makes it subject to criteria of intelligibility and rationality. It is this characteristic which permits proof of the inconsistency of discrimination arising in disrespect. (3) Attitudes and emotion do, however, derive from feelings which lack any cognitive or evaluative component, and an account of this relationship does much to clarify the social character of the imperatives of moral reason.

The Metaphysics of Morals

To assign several of the matters discussed here to metaphysics of morals is to distinguish them from the concerns of metaethics, which has to do with narrow logical and linguistic points, and from those of ethics itself, which is concerned with the truth and confirmation of evaluative judgments. Whereas metaethics is concerned with questions of logical modality and ethics with formally contingent statements, what may be alternatively titled "metaphysical ethics" deals with conceptual stringencies of intermediate strength. The nature of these stringencies may be initially suggested by analogy with recent work in metaphysics proper and in philosophical logic.

If the descriptive metaphysicians are right to deny that all necessity is logical necessity, then there should be propositions which, though they express logical possibilities, it would be irrational to affirm, or somehow impossible to assert intelligibly. It can be plausibly argued, for example, that given the way in which one acquires the concept of a person, it would be irrational to doubt the existence of other selves even though the solipsistic suggestion is neither self-contradictory nor meaningless and must therefore be considered to express a logical possibility. One might also reasonably expect to find statements in the prevailing scheme of values which, while not logically necessary, are as undeniable as statements concerning the basic features of the prevailing metaphysical scheme. These points and their significance can be well illustrated by various kinds of naturalistic theories of value.

Ethical naturalism—here understood to include any view according to which some irreducibly evaluative property is coextensive with some natural one—is clearly to be distinguished from metaethical naturalism—according to which the properties in question are necessarily coextensive, they being identical or the words for them being synonymous. It is clear that discovery of some specific property-identity or case of synonymity would entail the truth of the corresponding statement of ethical naturalism, but the falsity of metaethical naturalism would in no way impede the weaker view. Moore, after all, was an ethical naturalist, and the work of Charles Baylis and others who have resisted the lure of linguistic analysis shows that naturalism of this modest type can be maintained whatever the conclusions of metaethics. To be sure, security from logical assault reflects an inherent weakness in such views. Statements of the form, "Such-and-such is capable of being admired," are apparently not subject to empirical proof and can be supported only indirectly and inconclusively by reference to their factual counterparts. That something is admired provides some indication that it is worthy of being admired, but the weight of that evidence can be increased, never made conclusive, by weighing various testimony in appropriate ways, taking into account peculiar attachments, mental aberrations, and so on. Although the procedure is entirely practicable, therefore, it leaves the most obvious truths merely probable, and does not account for the fact that, for example, the admirability of some qualities could hardly be denied. Merely empirical systems, as Kant complained, want brain, and moralists want to show that such systems can be supplemented by rational principles which make their propositions undeniable. Such undeniability is a characteristic feature of propositions expressing metaphysical beliefs, and it can be shown that a proposition of metaphysical ethics can in virtue of this property be employed to deduce the sort of result obtained inductively by ethical naturalism.

Statements are undeniable if it is necessarily the case that given satisfaction of certain perspicuous conditions they are true, and doubt about what is undeniable in this sense is an obvious form of irrationality. There are a number of species of undeniability, two of which have particular interest. A statement may be said to be pragmatically undeniable if what it asserts it also expresses, and pragmatic paradoxes, unassertible statements, result when what is asserted contradicts what is expressed. "The cat is on the mat and I believe it" is undeniable in this sense, and "The cat is on the mat and I don't believe it" is unassertible because any assertion of the first conjunct expresses what the second conjunct denies. For the same reason, assertion of "The cat is on the mat" pragmatically implies "I believe that the cat is on the mat." Such implication is distinguished from logical implication by the possibility that it be true when the assertion (or "antecedent") is true and the proposition expressed in that assertion (the "consequent") is false. The difference between what one says and what one means to convey in saying it puts liars in danger of inadvertent veracity. The same distinction governs the very similar implication of "I have an obligation" by an assertion (or performance) of "I promise." In promising one expresses an obligation without necessarily accepting one in any sense not definable in brute terms of nonfulfillment and possibility of unpleasant consequences, so that it is possible to make perfectly good promises without accepting any norm just as it is possible to make perfectly good assertions without believing what one says. Both of these things are evident from the analysis of pragmatic implication and undeniability. The condition imposed upon the situations in question is evidently sincerity: assertion of *"p"* pragmatically implies "I believe *p*" if and only if it is undeniable given that assertion that I believe *p*; which is to say that necessarily, if I am sincere, then if I assert *p* I believe it. Analogous remarks could be made about promising and obligation, and it is obvious on this analysis that failure to satisfy the condition of sincerity in no way renders an assertion or promise defective. Only explicit denial of what an assertion or a promise expresses does that.

It is also possible to identify a semantical species of undeniability and implication. Without thereby pretending to assess the respective merits of the theories of descriptions and presuppositions, it is legitimate to say that "All dogs bark" semantically implies "There are dogs" and that, given that all dogs bark, "There are dogs" is undeniable without special explanation. Semantical implication and undeniability, like their pragmatic counterparts, have to do with what is ordinarily indicated rather than explicitly said in making a statement, but in this case the falsity of what is so indicated renders the statement in question truth-valueless. Again like the pragmatic relations, however, the semantical ones remain unaffected by such falsity. This, too, is evident upon analysis. The semantical modalities are so called because they are governed by the condition that ostensible referring terms be genuine, and the above sentences may be expressed in this way: "Necessarily, if 'dogs' refers, then if all dogs bark there are dogs." This is true whether or not the condition of reference is satisfied.

Just as there are near relatives to pragmatic implication in statements about practices, there are interesting analogues of semantical implication in statements about emotion and evaluation. It is undeniable that if something is dangerous it is fear worthy and it would be absurd to say, "That is dangerous but not worthy of fear." The sentence is not contradictory, however. For something cannot be fear worthy if no one has the capacity to fear it any more than it ought to be feared if it cannot be, and no matter how dangerous something may be there might be no one capable of fearing it. The sentence is nevertheless absurd because its intelligibility indicates that the capacity exists: if it did not, fear could not be identified. When this condition is put explicitly the sentence can be expressed as the necessary truth, "If something is feared, then if it is dangerous it is fear worthy." Quite analogous remarks can be made about the sentence, "If something is superior, it is admirable," which may be expressed, "If something is admired, then if it is superior it is admirable." Since it is merely a matter of observation whether someone is superior in strength or honesty and whether these qualities are admired, statements typical of ethical naturalism can be more easily and more decisively confirmed through the metaphysics of value than by empirical generalization. Metaphysics in this unobjectionable sense restores what logical investigation overlooks and what empirical investigation cannot reach.

If these remarks are correct and the distinctions genuine then a confusion frequently attributed to naturalists — the assimilation of normative concepts such as admirability to dispositional concepts — is improperly ascribed. That something is admired shows, of course, that it is capable of being admired, not that it is worthy of being admired, but the missing connection between the two concepts of admirability can be readily supplied through reference to a discernible superiority, just as reference to danger supplies the connection between fear and fearworthiness. To be sure, this incautious statement ignores important problems, the most interesting of which concern such attitudes as admiration for "superior mendacity." The intelligibility of these expressions shows that they denote logically possible objects of admiration, but their oddity indicates that the possibility is real only for oddly constituted societies. This suggestion is confirmed in a concluding discussion about adequate tests for judgments about admirability and the like which shows how this quality is related to general agreement about what is worthy of admiration. The point to be made here, however, is merely that although metaethical naturalism is surely false, metaphysical naturalism simply expresses those conditions, or capacities, without which there would be no value: the capacity to fear, to admire, and the like. The way in which such capacities govern evaluative reasoning is well illustrated by the interplay of respect and disrespect for persons characteristic of discrimination.

Disrespect

The acts of discrimination of most interest to moralists are those which indicate an attitude of disrespect towards the persons affected. Not all such acts have this quality. Discrimination in favor of certain persons need indicate no disrespectful attitude towards others; of two equally well qualified candidates, an employer may choose his cousin without prejudice to the other. Since, however, arguments about discrimination-against do not necessarily apply to discrimination-in-favor-of, "discrimination" will always be used in the former sense. Even acts of discrimination in this sense may fail to indicate disrespect. Among these are acts based upon false belief, such as an error about the abilities of members of certain groups, and actions required of benign officials encharged with the enforcement of discriminatory policies. Of course, such policies themselves often originate in error or contempt, and, apart from policies having inadvertently discriminatory consequences, all acts of discrimination express a belief on the part of those ultimately responsible for them that the victims are inferior in some respect which involves the lack of certain rights. Such beliefs are, by definition, false — if they were true the behavior in question would be not discriminatory but differential — but unless the error is itself inexcusable the person acting from these beliefs need not be blameworthy. It is something very close to inexcusable error, however, which distinguishes cases of discrimination founded in disrespect. They, too, involve beliefs about inferiority — without them the attitude would not make sense — but as well as being false they are in these cases necessarily false. They may be found to be conjoined with true beliefs which contradict them.

The irrationality of culpable discrimination can be explicated in terms of a simple if somewhat schematic account of relationships between attitudes, behavior, beliefs, and the intelligibility and justification of each. Attitudes, emotion, and the like are causal factors in significant human behavior. Fear may make one run, disrespect make one treat another in unusual ways. Such emotions and attitudes can exist, however, only in connection with beliefs — a belief about danger in the case of fear, about inferiority in the case of disrespect — without which human behavior would lack conscious reasons, and distinctions between running and fleeing, differential treatment and discrimination, would be impossible. The beliefs which support attitudes must, furthermore, be justified (though they need not be true) if those attitudes themselves are to be called justified, appropriate, or rational. Although fear of something only apparently dangerous is rational, fear of something obviously benign is not. In making this point it is not necessary to disagree with those who point out, quite rightly, that it is logically possible for any attitude or emotion to attach to any object; attitudes and emotions need not be rational in order to be intelligible. People can be of two minds about things, realizing that they are safe while believing also that danger exists, and the one belief may make the emotion of fear intelligible while conjunction with the other renders it irrational. This is precisely what characterizes disrespectful discrimination. Such behavior is made intelligible and purportedly rational by a belief; it is shown to be irrational by the priority of a contradictory belief.

The basic inference of a discriminatory judgment can be represented in this way: from possession of a certain property there follows an inferiority of worth. Having a certain property implies in some sense being relevantly inferior. Not every such inference is discriminatory. The property in question may be a natural characteristic, a conventional status, or a moral property, and in any of these cases differential treatment may well be logically faultless. Deficiencies in virtue (cowardice, dishonesty, cruelty, and the like) may make one deserving of disrespect and excuse the intolerance of or punishment by others. Possession of a natural property (a certain age, sex, or color, for example) or a difference in rank, whether conventional (birth, wealth, schooling) or natural (strength, agility, learning) may unfit one to perform a selected task, and one has no right to positions for which he lacks the qualifications. Of course, to infer from one's possession of such a property that he has inferior worth with respect to a given task may be invalid. Job discrimination against women and the elderly may represent careless generalizations, but such cases are relatively uninteresting, since lack of respect for one's crate-moving abilities, for example, does not properly lead to differential treatment in matters unrelated to the imputed deficiency. It is relatively easy, furthermore, to deflect charges of discrimination in such cases by reference to custom or legislation which describes differential treatment of women as "protection" rather than "discrimination" or disposes of the problem of the elderly through establishment of a somewhat arbitrary "retirement age." This is not at all to deny that conclusive cases against the injustice of such measures can sometimes be formulated. It is only to set such examples aside on the grounds that the conclusiveness of these cases derives from reference to facts which have to do with social expediency and the temper of the times rather than from the formal inconsistency of clearly discriminatory judgments. This kind of inconsistency occurs in inferences from possession of some status or natural property to inferiority of a moral kind.

It is undeniable that if one has some moral vice then there is a sense in which that person is worthy of disrespect. It might be maintained that someone could also find it undeniable that anyone with a given nonmoral property was morally inferior and ensconce himself by this means in a logically impregnable position. Metaethical noncognitivists have a view which permits this but it mistakes the nature of undeniability. The form of argument by which this may be shown is usefully introduced through consideration of the stronger (and probably contrary to fact) supposition that the mistake in a discriminatory judgment resides in believing that the relationship between possession of some nonmoral property and moral inferiority is one of logical implication. Because such inferences are invalid it would be logically possible for the discriminator to believe truly that one might have the characteristic in question yet not be inferior, even if he claims not to believe it. It can be argued that from this logical possibility and some defensible assumptions it follows that the discriminator has not merely made a logical mistake but that he has inconsistent beliefs as well. The result can be derived from the use of a simple principle which, though unacceptable without certain restrictions, may be made entirely plausible by means of admissible emendations: If it is logically possible that a certain person believe that something is the case, then that person believes it logically possible that this is the case. If, then, it is logically possible that a discriminator believe a person to have any given nonmoral characteristic yet not be relevantly inferior, he believes it logically possible that this is the case, and this belief contradicts the belief, expressed in the discriminatory judgment, that the victim is inferior in virtue of some such property.

The possibility of belief does not, of course, in general imply belief that something is possible. There are a number of evident counterexamples. (1) It is logically possible to believe both that a situation is dangerous and to believe that it is not, but no one would believe it possible that a situation is and is not dangerous. (2) It was logically possible for Fermat to believe his "Last Theorem" false, but he did not believe it possible for it to be false; he believed he had a proof to the contrary. (3) It is possible for an Eskimo to believe that there are kangaroos, but an Eskimo need not believe it possible that there are kangaroos, since an Eskimo need not know anything about kangaroos. (4) Even if it is possible that one believe Aristotle to have tutored Alexander one may not believe that this is possible, for he need not know those names. Such examples show that the epistemic analogue of "Barcan's Formula" here in question cannot be accepted without certain restrictions. The qualifications needed in the present case are evident: what is believed must be (i) consistent, (ii) contingent, (iii) free of unknown concepts, (iv) devoid of singular referring terms. To these it may be added that the belief must not be inordinately complex and need not be presently entertained. The other restrictions, however, are the operative ones and together amount to a synthetic principle of rationality and conceptual adequacy which says, in effect, that anyone who can formulate an intelligible, contingent proposition recognizes that it expresses a logical possibility. Not to know this would be not to know the language in which the propositions were formulated, and assuming the existence of such knowledge permits one to move from the antecedent of the rule, which expresses a possibility, to the consequent, which expresses a fact. Because it is based upon a synthetic but innocuous assumption about linguistic ability the rule in question seems unobjectionable and unavoidable in a way not true of undesirable principles of modal logic.

That any rational person believes logically possible what one's conceptual apparatus makes it logically possible for him to believe implies that the hypothetical discriminator described here is not such a person. For if it is the case that the discriminator believes it logically impossible that anyone with a certain property be inferior yet it is logically possible for him to believe otherwise, then in virtue of the rule just described he believes it logically possible that someone have the property in question yet not be inferior. Since this belief contradicts the other, he has logically inconsistent beliefs, and since the latter belief is one which any suitably endowed creature must have, it is the belief expressed in the original behavior which must be rejected and that behavior considered irrational.

It is doubtful that any discriminator has made this particular error, and the characterization of the discriminator's reasoning should be improved and his position strengthened by weakening the sense of implication involved. It must not be made so weak that his thoughts become unintelligible. In particular it must not depend on a simply "criterial" connection between evaluative judgments and natural properties which serve as criteria for those evaluations in any sense of "criteria" which permits them to be assigned simply according to the preferences of the person employing them. Blameworthy discrimination is differential behavior originating in an attitude of disrespect which is supported by a belief in the inferiority of its object, and it is fairly clear that a decision to treat certain properties as criteria of inferiority is insufficient to account for disrespect. A preference for black skin is not enough to make disrespect for those with white intelligible, since the attitude is inseparable from notions about desert and desert is not determined by preference.

To have decided attitudes is to have not just preferences but ideals. Opinions about desert may be traced to some ideal of what it is to be a person, such that to fall short of the ideal is to be relevantly inferior, and such an ideal may render one incapable of imagining that anyone failing to meet it might not be inferior. In the grip of such an ideal one may find it simply undeniable that certain persons are inferior, and slavery to this prejudice frees one, at least provisionally, from the absurdity of the commitment sketched above. Since undeniability is formally analogous to logical necessity the desired pattern of implication is preserved while the relative weakness of the concept seems to protect one who finds certain evaluative judgments undeniable from the naturalistic errors associated with the stronger modality. This sort of implication would seem, furthermore, accurately to characterize the discriminator's pattern of thought. For whereas it is difficult to imagine circumstances in which one might come to hold there to be a relevant logical relationship between obviously disparate properties it is quite easy to think of someone finding it undeniable, or unimaginable, that a person with a given manifest characteristic could be anything but morally inferior.

This defense is logically very strong, for a difficulty faces any attempt at immediate extension of the previous argument to the case of undeniability. It is tempting to argue in this way: "By hypothesis, one believes it undeniable that a person is inferior if that person has a certain nonmoral characteristic. Alternatively expressed, one believes it unassertible, or unimaginable, that a person have the characteristic in question and not be inferior. By the rationality rule, furthermore, one believes it logically possible that someone with this characteristic not be inferior. Linguistic competence, however, surely permits the assumption that the logical possibility of a proposition's truth carries the assertibility of the proposition with it, and with this assumption the desired result follows immediately. One believes, inconsistently, both that it is unassertible that a person with a certain property is not inferior and that the same proposition is assertible." In fact, it is not obvious that linguistic competence does permit the crucial assumption. The beliefs which constitute the premises of the argument are formally consistent, since the logical possibility of a proposition's truth does not always carry assertibility with it. Were this not the case there would be no descriptive metaphysics and no pragmatic paradoxes. Nevertheless, the desired conclusion can be derived. For the possibility in question does not belong to any conceptually problematical class of propositions but to one for which there is no interesting distinction between possibility and assertibility. This distinction marks a difference only in special sorts of cases, and the relationship between moral and nonmoral properties is too distant to make it one of these. Because this is so, linguistic competence may for the case in question be taken to indicate belief in the assertibility of propositions believed logically possible, and the previously mentioned argument may be accepted. The disrespect which sustains the belief in inferiority which in turn makes that attitude intelligible is thus shown to be irrational — as is the behavior caused by that attitude.

Several points should be made about this argument in order to avoid misunderstanding. The rationality rule upon which it is based might seem objectionable if the great weakness of the concept of logical possibility is unappreciated. The rule is in any case employed in order to effect a formal proof and could be dispensed with in an informal treatment in terms of good reasons for belief. Nevertheless, it is intended simply to reflect the fact that ability to use a language involves ability to recognize the presence or absence of simple logical relations and it is such relations to which the intensity of the discriminator's attitude blinds him. It may be added that even if such fanaticism were nonexistent — a suggestion encouraged by the availability of reasonable argument in support of unreasonable attitudes — its very possibility indicates that reason holds tighter rein on emotion than has sometimes been thought possible.

On the other hand, possession of reason does not alone account for the existence of a moral sense, and the argument given here does not constitute the derivation of an evaluative conclusion from non-evaluative premises. Irrationality provides no reason to avoid disrespect unless rationality is considered valuable, and persons not at peace with the world may doubt its usefulness. Indeed, it has been suggested that even in philosophy substantial reputations can be gained by seriously maintaining propositions which are obviously false, and this observation permits the present point to be made in a somewhat more interesting way. For it has also been said that the oddity of such propositions is that, though intelligible, they can be formulated only within a context of understandings to the contrary, and it is just such a feature which prevents one from saying that the irrationality of discrimination can be proven outside a context of such understandings. Disrespect is a moral attitude and involves imbuing others with a moral status, albeit an inferior one involving absence of moral rights. It presupposes, therefore, the ability to reason morally, that is, to reason about moral qualities such as honesty, kindness, and the like. Hence one cannot discriminate, deny rights, at all unless one is able to employ concepts of moral virtues. One might actually lack this ability if he suffered from a kind of emotional impoverishment in which the attitudes of respect and disrespect could not be formed. In such a state one could not be said to be in any sense irrational, and if reason is not the slave of the passions neither does it determine attitudes.

Since one may be rational without reasoning morally it is clear that no condemnation of discrimination by itself places any general prohibitions upon behavior or determines any substantive rights. On the other hand, if one does recognize the irrationality of discrimination based upon moral disrespect then one grants the need for one kind of respect for persons. To avoid unwarrantedly differential treatment of certain persons is to permit all persons to pursue their legitimate aims and interests unimpeded by special restrictions. Such respect for persons, nevertheless, guarantees its objects neither success nor any particular assistance in the realization of these interests. Moral rationality involves no imperative to promote material equality or to be benevolent. To be sure, to refrain from kindnesses may be socially uncomfortable and the emotional impoverishment making one unable to be particularly kind may demonstrate (if only in retrospect) the preferability of benevolence to its alternatives, but this is simply to say that real concern for other persons is encouraged by practical reason and is not logically incumbent upon those who reason morally any more than upon those who do not. These commonplaces can be misunderstood, however, and deserve additional comment.

Respect for Persons

The expression "respect for persons" has a number of possible significations. Usually it indicates an attitude of consideration for the interests of persons in general, one based upon the belief that the interests of others are as legitimate as one's own. However, the phrase might also be used to indicate an attitude of admiration for specific persons and be associated with belief in the superiority of its object. This is a moral attitude based upon beliefs concerning moral qualities and is to be distinguished from the related nonmoral attitude based upon beliefs concerning physical properties, status, and the like. Whereas admiration for a person's courage amounts to respect for that person (at least with regard to that quality), admiration for someone's physical strength does not amount to respect for that person, even though the two sorts of attitudes are closely related and subject to popular confusion. "Respect for persons" may, finally, indicate a variety of mental behavior ranging from prudent forethought to minimize risk in dealings with others to sympathetic regard for other's goals and interests. Unlike attitudes of respect, the desires and sentiments characteristic of respect of this latter sort do not require support by beliefs about worth. Neither forbearance from trespass nor benevolent assistance have any implications about the merits of their beneficiaries. Theologians make the same point about divine grace.

Corresponding distinctions should be observed in the case of "disrespect," which may indicate a general attitude of contemptuous disregard for others and the withholding from them of rights demanded for oneself, a similar attitude about certain persons arising in discernment of specific moral failings, or merely that carelessness or unconcern about others which results in unwitting or unconscionable intrusiveness. It has often been argued that such disrespectful behavior violates imperatives of practical reason: since bitter experience quickly makes one aware of the undesirability of that behavior, one ought to develop a disposition to cooperation or at least to noninterference as a means of securing desires. Clearly, however, experience might cause one to sink instead into a state of apathy or indifference, to give up those desires and cease acting at all. A similar qualification should be made to the observation that acknowledging the irrationality of discriminatory attitudes amounts to having an attitude of respect for persons. For, having been convinced of the irrationality of discrimination, one might conceivably adopt a neutral attitude of indifference in which various virtues and vices are still recognized but no longer arouse admiration or contempt; one might, that is, give up previous moral beliefs and come to withhold not simply moral rights but even moral status from all persons.

This structural similarity between prudential and "attitudinal" models of human interaction suggests a more significant connection between them, the nature of which is indicated by the situations to which they apply. Although the former view, being based upon noncognitive states, necessarily omits the attitudes characteristic of moral reasoning, it is useful for understanding childhood and periods of poor social cohesion in which people act as creatures of caution, considering other men "means" or potential antagonists rather than "ends" or fellow beings. The alternative model, by contrast, is more adequate to mature persons and relatively untroubled civilizations, and the attitude of respect bears a similar relationship to its prudential variant. It is natural, therefore, to conceive of respect for persons as the end result of a development process the almost inevitable initiation of which explains the infrequency of indifference to others, or the fact that one's concept of a person so readily acquires a moral dimension.

The lineaments of normal moral ontogeny are familiar. The child, far from being father of the man, is generally much less reluctant to steal, lie, cheat and otherwise defy convention than his elders. He lacks admiration for common qualities and virtues and has a more external than pious respect for the forms of the society in which he finds himself. Respecting others only in the sense of being wary of their power, he is deterred from breaking social rules by fear of harm rather than by any natural desire to observe them. Ordinarily, however, he becomes increasingly familiar with his group and increasingly aware of his own place in it. He understands and appropriates the criteria determining the importance of various natural and moral properties and comes to admire and respect those who have them. The process of progressing in this way from disrespectful to respectful behavior and eventually to attitudes of admiration and respect is not implausibly described as one of self-discovery. It is the development of a self-concept, one which is necessarily evaluative because it has to do with the presence or absence of properties of one's-self considered important by other persons.

Respect for some is not the same as respect for all. Within a given group, the first is a kind of admiration, based upon belief in the superiority of a person's moral qualities, the second a kind of tolerance based upon belief in the equality of moral rights. Relativization to groups suggests, however, a question, not explicitly considered heretofore, about the possibility of selective tolerance as well as selective admiration. It is clear that attitudes based upon beliefs about properties peculiar to members of one's own group can amount to respect only for persons with the characteristics in question, and there is a tendency towards disrespect or indifference to those outside whatever one considers one's group. That is, outsiders may be considered morally deficient or lacking moral status altogether. The first of these attitudes may be quite reasonable. Societies have characteristic values and naturally value qualities characteristic of their members. If, for example, martial virtues are especially admired in a society, its very survival is likely to indicate possession by contiguous groups. Members of a business community may similarly take pride in their scrupulousness while having a certain disdain for the careless honesty of those with whom they deal. Even within one's society, of course, certain persons will be deficient in certain respects, but they, like outsiders, may still be extended moral status and that respect which is a form of tolerance. In all such cases respect for persons is required by the assignment of moral properties to them, but these properties need not be ones which inspire admiration. What, however, of a people who withheld moral status from outsiders altogether, thinking questions of moral rights and moral properties not to arise for such persons? Outsiders in this case would be considered morally equivalent to animals, and to treat them as such would, therefore, be merely to manifest a discriminatory pattern of behavior. It would not be to discriminate because in the absence of moral status any reason is a sufficient reason for differential treatment. Of course, the behavior must not originate in disrespect, for that is a denial of indifference, but this leaves one free to say that indifference is in fact the characteristic attitude behind behavior termed (by the victim or other person who accords him moral status) "discrimination."

The suggestion that charges of discrimination are merely ethnocentric and indicate acceptance of conventional rights not granted by the "discriminator" cannot, however, be maintained. If one assigns a moral property to any person one must be prepared to estimate the extent to which anything identifiable as a person has it. If one admires honesty he must be able to ask of any person whether he is honest or not, and to have this ability is effectively to grant moral status to all persons. Indifference in such cases is intelligible only as a disguise for disrespect. Of course, social factors can help disguise one's common humanity even from oneself, but these remarks are intended not so much to reiterate the possibility of irrationality in historical societies as to preface an explanation of how an attitude of admiration can arise from simple feelings, how such an attitude can be a form of moral respect, and how, therefore, an attitude of respect becomes generalizable.

Social forces are clearly superable. Although the possibility of a liberal morality seems largely contingent upon factors weakening the significance of membership in relatively circumscribed groups, many persons in many ages for which the characteristic attitude of respect was dangerously unconventional have managed to develop it. Indeed, although the development of an attitude of respect for persons is not inevitable and in the wrong circumstances is not easy, it can, without further abuse to the word, be considered natural. Most men possess a capacity for reason and experience. Most possess as well the capacity to be struck or impressed by certain experiences and to adopt an attitude of interest in answering the question, "What makes that striking?" Since, furthermore, what is striking is ordinarily a departure from what is familiar or usual, the attitude of interest depends upon the intimate relationship between present and past experience in the context of which the phenomenon in question is unexpected or inexplicable. One's cumulative experience thus helps to determine what one is interested in, what is interesting-to-oneself. Experience, however, can be not only cumulative but also collective, and reference to the latter makes it possible to distinguish those phenomena which are interesting without qualification from those merely interesting to particular persons. Any of a number of considerations shows that this distinction is genuine and that the unrestricted term is the fundamental one. The logically subordinate role of interest-to-oneself is evident, for example, from the observation that to show someone that something is uninteresting is to make it cease to be interesting-to-him. The demonstration fills the deficiency in experience that made the phenomenon in question striking. To be interesting is to be worthy of interest, and to be worthy of interest is to be appropriately related to a given fund of knowledge — a fund which is for the greater part in the keeping of the community. Only for the greater part, however. The knowledge of the specialist may make him uniquely qualified to determine the interest of a phenomenon, for it may make him able to appreciate matters which seem uninteresting to others until they are given sufficient background to understand their significance. Nevertheless, it is the potentially public nature of the knowledge in question which makes it the test of interestingness.

Much the same remarks can be made of admiration in general and of moral respect in particular. Admiration derives from such feelings as astonishment and the wariness of merely prudential respect and involves identification of features which produce it. As in the case of interest, these features may support the judgment that something is admirable (worthy of admiration) or simply admirable-to-oneself (admired), the difference resting primarily upon communal consensus arising from experience. In this case, too, additional information may result in changes of attitude. Just as something interesting may become something simply expected as it becomes familiar or understood, something once worthy of admiration may lose this dignity as it becomes commonplace, and something worthy of respect may cease to be particularly virtuous and become expected in a moral sense, obligatory. The significance of the similarity between admiration and respect is obvious. There is no important difference between being impressed by and coming to admire unusual physical strength and being struck by and coming to admire unusual honesty. The one is as natural and as normal as the other. Anyone who has attitudes at all is likely to have moral attitudes, the correctness of which is subject to the test of collective experience. It is this test, of course, which discourages admiration for such things as superior weakness or superior dishonesty. Since such qualities can be determined not to be admirable, their ranking among others is too low to make the term "superior" appropriate for them. Different societies, however, may have different tests, and it is perhaps possible for there to be groups admiring of qualities which could only be described in this odd way.

There is to be no discussion here of the curiosities of the fact that although moral beings are social beings there may be somewhat different societies and somewhat different conceptions of moral worth. Nor will it be inquired whether social beings are necessarily moral or whether there might be a viable society based upon aesthetic or religious sensitivity and in which human relations were conducted by prudence alone. It may simply be noted that the human emotional repertoire prevents this from happening and that existence of that repertoire makes it false to suggest that intersocietal moral differences indicate that morality is merely a conventional institution or set of characteristic principles. Moral judgments depend not upon derivation from moral principles established in a logically arbitrary way but upon the discernment of moral qualities the admirability of which derives from the collective experience of a community. It is possible to exaggerate the limitations which this fact places upon moral autonomy, for one's personal experience may result in various forms of eccentricity in evaluation which are tolerated within wide limits. If respect for the interests of other persons does not lie within these limits, opinions about how such respect is to be supplemented by cooperation with and assistance to others in the furtherance of those interests do lie within them. Even if one admires benevolence and self-sacrifice, for example, the qualities admired need constitute no obligation for the admirer. For those qualities are virtues, and virtues are moral qualities the possession of which is not expected. They contrast with vices, which one is expected to avoid. Whereas marked cruelty is intolerable, special kindness is not required; and whereas discrimination is prohibited, one is still permitted choice of neighbors and has no obligation to risk personal loss by ignoring the attitudes of a restrictive community. Matters of active concern for others are ones of sentiment and personal decision and questions concerning them cannot be answered by studies in the metaphysics of morals.

Osborne on the Art of
Appreciation

Paul Welsh
Duke University

Harold Osborne holds that the appreciation of the arts is a skill.[1] He appears also to maintain it is possible to give an account of this skill that will apply to all the arts, not simply to a particular art. The account, moreover, is to tell "an interested and intelligent person" how he would set about acquiring this skill.

To possess a skill is at least to possess an ability to "do some thing," whether it is to make cabinets, or to discriminate false from genuine attributions, or perhaps, to tell Assam from Ceylon tea. Now on Osborne's account, skill in appreciation of the arts appears to result in the production of an "aesthetic object." But unlike other skills, the results of this activity are not easily assessed. It is not even clear that it will be sensible to praise (or fault) the exerciser of this skill.

I want in this paper to look at Osborne's account. I think he is in fact doing something rather different than he claims to. The "skill" he describes is not a skill, and the "object" to which it is directed is not the product of a skill, if it is a product at all.

I

The skill which Osborne claims is required for appreciation of the arts is the "ability to apprehend complex organizations of visual and auditory wholes and the recondite overall qualities of such wholes" (p. 8). That art deals with complex wholes and that there are such "overall" qualities does not seem for Osborne to require much justification. But the characterization of the latter is worth noting. The beauty which the connoisseur apprehends "cannot be described in aesthetic categories because it belongs uniquely to the aesthetic construct" (p. 13). Sometimes, however, a modified claim is put forward. The qualities of works of art outrun the

---

1. *The Art of Appreciation* (Oxford, 1970), p. 2.

vocabulary we possess. In either case, "cognitive apprehension" of an art work is ruled out.

All right, then. How do we develop the skill? What must we do? The answer we get is one which puts off the question. "Skill," we are told, involves two sorts of competence. One who can play chess knows the rules of the game. This is a kind of competence. But we can also talk of degrees of skill, in the sense in which one player is better than another. Here the skillful player, like the skillful artist, cannot tell you exactly how his strategy occurs to him, how he achieves the results he does. So, too, the connoisseur may not be able to specify what he does in appreciating works of art. Nor, says Osborne, should we find this surprising. A faculty which deals with nondiscursive matters — presumably, apprehending the qualities of a work of art is nondiscursive — is not wholly amenable to description and analysis.

I want to ignore the two obvious nonsequiturs. That a "faculty" is "nondiscursive" does not entail that it cannot be described or analyzed. Nor does it follow that if an action is not rule-governed, it is not teachable. Osborne may, of course, be using "rule" loosely, as equivalent to method. But if this latter is true, he cannot claim that there is *no* method in appreciation without denying that there is a skill or art of appreciation. He can only claim that while there is an art, even the best practitioners cannot tell you how they achieve their results. But to take this refuge is to make a mystery of the skill. It is singular to tell a reader that the purpose of one's book is to show how the power of appreciation can be trained, and then to announce that what the aspirant must cultivate is the "latent knowledge and unspecifiable know-how which are the essence of any skill at all" (p. 7). The expert, apparently, may teach the novice by taking him under his wing, "provided the pupil himself has a natural flair," by example, percept, and general maxim. This seems to allow that the skill may be imparted, but not through a book. This is an odd claim in the light of Osborne's announced purpose.

II

"Skill" has more than one sense, of course. One sense which Osborne recognizes is a capacity for the performance of craft or practical task plus cleverness in doing it. He talks of a skilled craftsman, and of someone said to be skillful in a sport. These presumably require practice and training. But Osborne wants to talk also of "capacities for mental performances." His list of these is a little odd for it includes mathematical ability and the cultivation of mystical experience (p. 7). Some mental skills, he claims, are cognitive skills, e.g. wine-tasting and perfume-blending. Some persons require both practical and cognitive skills, for example, a concert performer. Artistic creation, however, is not a skill. Artistic appreciation is. The argument is that the capacity to create fine works just cannot be taught or imparted. This argument seems unpersuasive unless "capacity" is being used in some special way. Artists and architects, like the rest of us, require training and practice in their metier. And, on the other hand, some people are much better than others as critics. Their skill is not simply the result of training or instruction.

In any event, the skill which Osborne holds is involved in the art of appreciation is both a mental and a noncognitive skill. For explanation and clarification of this claim one turns naturally to what Osborne has written of appreciation.

III

Appreciation, he tells us, "is a complicated and many-sided activity" (p. 18). "Nevertheless, we are saying something to the point when we say that it is to be described in terms of taking up an aesthetic attitude to something rather than thinking analytically about it, or responding to it emotionally, or assessing its utility value" (p. 19). Most basic, to be aesthetically preoccupied is to apprehend it in a special kind of way. This he calls "percipience" (p. 19). "It involves the cultivation of awareness for its own sake" (p. 19).

Osborne moves rather bewilderingly in describing this skill. He describes it alternately as "taking up an aesthetic attitude," "aesthetically contemplating," "aesthetic percipience," "aesthetically experiencing" and "aesthetically apprehending." It is not easy, for example, to see how to take up an aesthetic attitude is equivalent to aesthetic contemplation or perceiving, or whether perceiving is equivalent to experiencing.

Osborne in fact seems to be running several things together. On the one hand he wants to say something on this order: the aesthetic interest, the aesthetic point of view, is to be contrasted with practical or scientific interests. This seems reasonable enough. Asking how much money an object costs, how much money a play is taking in, is not evaluating the thing in aesthetic terms.

But it would be odd, at least, to talk of economic contemplation, or economically experiencing an object. We don't "experience" anything economically, though we might be said to look at it from an economic or practical point of view. If there is an aesthetic mode of awareness, there is no economic mode. If taking the aesthetic attitude means taking an aesthetic point of view, this need not entail trying to contemplate an object in a certain sort of way, though it does seem to mean ruling out some interests as irrelevant, and adopting certain criteria in assessing an object. It is not a mode of perception, nor, more importantly, is it a skill. Taking, say, a military, or practical point of view, is not something that we are either good at, or bad at, or can improve in.

Aesthetic contemplation, or "percipience," on the other hand is, as Osborne describes it, fixing attention on presented object. It is a form of absorption. When "absorption is achieved there is a loss of subjective time-sense, a loss of the sense of place and a loss of bodily consciousness" (p. 35). But since he recognizes that we may as easily be absorbed in a puzzle or piece of research, what we have yet is only a characterization of what it is to be absorbed. Aesthetic absorption is simply being absorbed with aesthetic objects. Is the absorption to be defended as aesthetic because of something we do, or something in the nature of the object? I've suggested that it's not helpful to be told that in aesthetic absorption we take the aesthetic attitude. Osborne claims we can take an aesthetic attitude towards anything. But until he tells us what the aesthetic interest is, or the criteria by which we determine aesthetic objects, we will not know what aesthetic absorption is, and whether one can, on his account, make any object the object of aesthetic absorption.

IV

Osborne claims that "in ordinary life we don't notice the perceptual qualities beyond what is necessary to recognize, classify and place them" (p. 21). It is the familiar picture drawn for us of a busy, hurrying people, driven by practical concerns, only giving half an eye to the world around us. In aesthetic perception we look at things for their own sake. Osborne also makes the claim that *what* we perceive is different. In nonaesthetic perception we are "aware of generalized and indeterminate perceptual qualities" (p. 21). When we look at things for their own sake the indeterminate qualities "become more precise and determinate." The "perceptual object" changes (p. 22).

Classifying "percipience" as nonutilitarian, I have suggested, may be a way of setting off an aesthetic interest from a nonaesthetic interest, but it is not obvious that perception can be classified in this way. A clinician may look very carefully at an X-ray, a sample of blood, a bit of tissue. Intense concern with the quality or property of a thing is not incompatible with a practical interest. Osborne himself notes that a craftsman or even a connoisseur may savor the qualities of the material he works with or is scrutinizing. Here are some examples Osborne offers:

Noting the rainbow sheen ruffing a pigeon's neck
The rhythmic rise and fall of susurration on a summer's day

The smoky calligraphies of wheeling birds
A clumsily pretentious cornice
The squat lugubrious block of the desk telephone

There is nothing in the examples Osborne gives us to help us determine whether aesthetic perception marks off a class of qualities, say, the
class of determinate and "particularized" qualities, such that any perception of them would count as aesthetic perception. The qualities noted
in aesthetic perception need not be veridical. If a tree "looks strong" and
I admire this appearance of strength, Osborne says, it does not matter
that the tree is in fact rotten. But this dubious example only runs together
perception and admiration, and serves only to widen the range of things
we may perceive aesthetically.

Osborne does seem to maintain that what makes the perception aesthetic is a heightening of alertness and acuity. He allows apparently that
this heightened perception may be induced by drugs. And it is tempting
to conclude that this is all that he ultimately means by percipience. This
sort of perception he describes as a "heightening" of perception, and
also as an "expansion" of awareness.

First of all, it is important in the content of Osborne's work to notice
that there is very little here that can be called a skill, or an art. It is a
capacity which can apparently be equally induced by drugs. It requires
only—at least on the account thus far—that we inhibit sentimental rev-
erie, inhibit practical concerns, and then hope for a heightened awareness
to take over. It does not seem to be something that we *do*.

It is not clear that Osborne would include in the range of aesthetic
percipience all or any sensory qualities. Does it include the smell of rotten
eggs, the scream of a crying child, the sound of a creaking door? Osborne
does want to make it clear that the awareness he describes need not be
pleasurable or linked with pleasure in any way. "When I take pleasure in
smelling a rose I am in a state of divided attention: half my attention is
on the smell, half is on the pleasure I am experiencing. But if I switch to
the state of percipience which I have called 'aesthetic', I become aware as
never before of the precise quality of the odour, and I dwell on its defac-
tory *quale;* if my attention is wholly engaged in percipience of the smell,
however momentarily, for just so long the awareness of its pleasantness
. . . recedes. I cease to be aware of pleasure" (p. 41).

To what then does one appeal to justify the activity? When we notice
the ruff of a pigeon's neck we may see something in its "true and unfamil-
iar being." But presumably this could occur without heightened awareness; and he also allows that if we look a second or third time, though
what we see may be exactly the quality of the object, the heightened
awareness may not be present. Instead, we can be bored, he says. Any-
how such objects lack complexity. And it is complex objects we require

for a sustained exercise of this capacity. We may put off for the moment, the question: why develop this skill?

We are not much clearer yet on why this form of percipience is called aesthetic. Osborne's answer seems to be that it is because it is directed to aesthetic qualities. And his reply to the question, What are aesthetic qualities? is this: "I shall regard as 'aesthetic qualities' any qualities which are of regular importance in our aesthetic commerce with works of art" (p. 61). This circular definition is, of course, unhelpful. Elsewhere Osborne classifies aesthetic qualities under the headings of sensory qualities, i.e. qualities of a single sensory mode, intersensory qualities, i.e. those which straddle more than one sensory mode, expressive qualities, those "which carry emotional implication," and formal qualities, such as unity and balance. Apart from the fact that the principle of classification is unclear, it is not obvious that noting, say, that a painting was unified would require either the discovery of a "precise" quality, or a heightening of awareness. Thus the relation between aesthetic qualities, percipience, and the skill required in appreciation needs to be made clear.

V

Aesthetic qualities are defined as qualities of aesthetic objects. But aesthetic objects are themselves first distinguished from works of art: Osborne classifies works of art as those which are "closely associated" with material things or "physical substrates," e.g. painting, sculpture, (p. 167) and "performances" which require time for their occurrence and appreciation, e.g. cinema, and music. Again, the principle of classification is unclear. At least the genus of which these two are species is obscure. What they have in common, Osborne tells us, is "that in order to be aware of a work fact it is necessary to attend to the existential substrate. Whether that is a material thing or a happening in a special sort of way" (p. 170). The aesthetic object is the artistic image which is actualized in awareness when an observer contemplates such a physical substrate aesthetically. "An 'aesthetic object' is a sub-class of 'perceptual' or 'phenomenal' objects. It comes into being when a suitable observer contemplates the physical substrate of a work of art in a suitable manner" (p. 171). However, it is quite possible, he says, to perceive a physical substrate without becoming aware of an aesthetic object (p. 171).

We seem then, in fact, to have three things: "physical" or existential substrates, perceptual objects, and aesthetic objects. The latter two belong together. But how a perceptual object—a painting?—differs from a physical object is a bit mystifying, unless we call the canvas, paint and frame the "physical substrate" of the perceptual object. But we should still be able to see the canvas, etc. And on the other side, calling an event, e.g. the performance of Hamlet, a perceptual object is a loose extension of "object." But this is not crucial. It is the nature of the aesthetic object and its relation to the work of art which is important.

Osborne begins with the disclaimer that he is not, in making these distinctions, subscribing to a particular philosophic theory or claim (p. 171). He claims to employ these terms as reasonably neat and concise descriptions of what we know at the level of experience. He takes himself to be giving a report of what is "common experience," and also something which is not a matter for debate.

It is a familiar and undebateable thing that we may look at a canvas, see it first as a puzzling and meaningless assemblage of unrelated areas and shapes, then find suddenly, without physical movement on our part that, "the shapes may cohere into an ordered and consistent system of interrelated patterns" (p. 172). So far, so good. But Osborne insists that it is crucial to understand that this "represents a real change in the object of vision." "It is not a matter of seeing the same visual object differently, as we may see different aspects of a material thing . . . the content of our visual field . . . has become different. And this may occur without any change in the material thing that is there before us" (p. 172).

Interestingly, Osborne allows that the same thing happens in ordinary experience. "Our ordinary perceptual experience is vague, imprecise and jejune" he tells us. The perceptual object of which we are aware is in many respects indeterminate. Again, we can look at a Van Gogh from close at hand and "see a welter of blots and streaks of pigment." At ten feet away we see an apple orchard. The same thing, he allows, holds for advertisement hoardings.

The facts Osborne points to are familiar enough. But there are two distinct things here. One is not noting the exact shape, or not distinguishing shade, hue, intensity and so on. The other is seeing patterns, becoming aware of the organization of shapes and colors where before we were not conscious of them. He wants to take these as two instances of the same thing. And he wants to hold that if we do not attend to the exact shape, it is incorrect to describe this as not noticing what we saw. Whatever we see, he claims, is a property of the "perceptual object." Vagueness, indeterminacy are properties of the perceptual object. If, later, we notice the "exact shape," we have a different perceptual object; one, for example, which is no longer indeterminate.

Again, some people may see a picture as a depiction—a field of such a site, with so many trees and so many cows, etc. Someone who also sees it as a pattern of shapes and forms sees a different visual object, one compatible with the first (p. 173).

I do not propose here to criticize in detail the theory of perception

Osborne offers us. I want to limit my observations as much as possible to what is relevant to the aesthetic theory he propounds. But it needs to be pointed out, I think, that his claim not to subscribe to a particular philosophical theory, is naive. It is not at all obvious that these terms are "neat and concise descriptions of which we know at the level of experience" (p. 171). At the very least, these are not neat and concise descriptions, nor are their nature and relations to one another easy to make out. Osborne is making the claim that perceptual objects have the properties we perceive them to have. As he puts it—"a visual experience is what it is in awareness" (p. 174).

If we look at his account of these three things—physical substrates, perceptual objects, and aesthetic objects—they turn out not to be three distinct things at all, and the grounds for distinguishing them prove shaky. Sometimes perceptual objects are said to be indeterminate objects. Some people, Osborne claims, are so uninterested in perceptual experience . . . that it is correct to describe their perceptual objects as permanently indeterminate. Aesthetic perception is said to render the indeterminate determinate. But a determinate perceptual object is quite possible: for example, an advertisement seen clearly. And it should presumably be an aesthetic object since "any single thing can become the object of an experience we call aesthetic" (p. 175).

But determinacy is not enough. An aesthetic object is better articulated, more fully determinate. Its shapes cohere in an "ordered and consistent system of interrelated patterns" (p. 172). "When we look at a picture as an aesthetic object we see it simultaneously *both* as the surface of a material thing and as a depiction having qualities not attributable to the material surface" (p. 176).

But now the aesthetic object is more than a perceptual object since the "physical picture surface" seen simply as the surface of a material object (pigmented canvas) contributes to the quality of an aesthetic object. "Its expressive influence is never absent when we see a work of art as an aesthetic object" (p. 177). "Aesthetic objects" now means a work of art seen in particular ways. Osborne allows that if two people look at a work of art one may see a perceptual object and the other an aesthetic object. And since someone looking at a work of art may also see the "physical surface" the function or role of the physical substrate becomes puzzling. It is always possible to perceive a physical substrate, he writes, without becoming aware of an aesthetic object. Do we then perceive perceptual objects? It seems possible, since all that is required is that we not look at it carefully. But the perceptual object is not the physical object, because Osborne allows that we can *compare* its qualities with the qualities of the physical stimulus which was its occasion (p. 174). But then perceptual objects could match exactly a physical object, and what the difference between them is, and what we should be comparing is a mystery. Osborne may be trying to take account of the fact that if we stand three inches away from a picture we see only blots of paint, that to see what is depicted we must step back from the picture. But in both cases we are either seeing perceptual objects or physical surfaces. Osborne's distinction has no ground. Or if a perceptual object is always indeterminate, so too are some oils and water colors. It is a fiction to claim that a painting is always determinate. And again, Osborne's distinction founders.

Osborne wants to hold that some people may look at works of art and yet not see aesthetic objects. These people, he claims, may be incapable of seeing aesthetic objects. But if it is possible to compare perceptual objects with their "physical stimulus," it ought, by the same token, to be possible to compare aesthetic objects with their physical stimulus and point out to those who can't see aesthetic objects what is missing in their perceptual objects. Or if this is not possible then we need to be told more about the status of works of art.

Sometimes, for Osborne, the work is an entity "which provides a more or less lasting possibility for a number of consumers to make actualizations (i.e. aesthetic objects) on the basis of the material thing . . . which [is] the existential substrate of the work of art" (p. 175). But it now appears that we cannot sensibly compare the aesthetic object with the work of art. There is, he claims, no single *correct* actualization although there may be *incorrect* actualizations. Thus it will not make sense to talk of comparing the aesthetic object with the work of art. Where we could on Osborne's view compare the perceptual object and its physical stimulus, we cannot compare the aesthetic object with the work of art. If then when two people look at a painting and one "sees" a perceptual object and the other an aesthetic object, then the aesthetic object cannot be explained simply in terms of what is seen. If two people with unimpaired sight look at a painting under similar physical conditions, and "see" two different objects, the difference cannot be simply in the seeing. And it seems clear that if this is true, telling someone to look again to "see" something he doesn't see will be pointless.

Competent observers, Osborne tells us, are those who can actualize correctly. It would be helpful to be told how this is done, and how one tells a correct from an incorrect actualization. This presumably is the skill which the art of appreciation is to teach. Instead we are told that it is excessively difficult to decide between conflicting judgments of taste, and that no precise rules can be given for the development of the power of appreciation (p. 186). More startling is the claim that "every time we attend seriously to a work of art for purposes of appreciation the aesthetic object which we actualize will be different in some respects from every previous time" (p. 219). This notion of perceptual novelty is one that not even Osborne himself maintains, for he also writes that when further performances [of a piece of music] no longer expand our apprehension by the revelation of new concretions we tend to become bored" (p. 183).

The skill which the competent observer possesses is not apparently something which needs much time for its exercise. "The experienced observer may from the start see the picture as a coherent aesthetic object" (p. 172), although apparently even this may be enriched by "a more complete apprehension of recondite aesthetic qualities" (p. 172). But none of this throws much light on the skill which is presumably the subject of Osborne's book.

What we find when we look further is rather a claim that aesthetic contemplation cannot in the nature of things be fully characterized, together with a definition of the aesthetic object which is, so to speak, a characterization of the goal the appreciation must reach. I shall begin first by giving an account of what an aesthetic object is for Osborne, and then look back again at the account of aesthetic contemplation and the skill it requires.

Osborne proposes to center his account of the aesthetic object principally on pictures, while urging that what he says of them applies without serious difficulty to other art forms. Of paintings, then, he says, "every picture exists as an organized configuration of flat patterns of lines and shapes in the picture plane or on planes very close to that of the canvas surface and simultaneously, as pattern in a notional three-dimensional picture space." "*Every* picture is an organization both of flat-pattern and of three-dimensional pattern in an illusory picture space, and every picture must be actualized in both modalities simultaneously" (p. 180). To this we must add "the sensory qualities of the material pigmented canvas" (p. 176). The physical appearance of the pigmented surface links intimately and inextricably with the aspect of the picture as depiction. "Aesthetically we must see the picture simultaneously as a configuration of textured surface, as a configuration of deep three-dimensional pattern; and the same pigmented area is seen differently as it forms part of various configurations" (p. 180). To use Osborne's vocabulary, these various modalities must be seen simultaneously as interlocking, as interrelated.

It is patent that what Osborne is doing is restating the old definition of a work of art. It is the familiar notion that works of art must be complex unities, except that the unification now is something the observer must in some way perform. And there seems no better reason for accepting it under this guise than any other. It would follow, of course, that a putative work of art that could not be so actualized would not be a work of art. It is also a consequence of this view, I think, that talks of degrees of unity, or more or less complex works, or of a work lacking unity but possessing aesthetic worth would not make sense.

Yet Osborne is clear that his definition will not fit all art forms. Some art forms by their nature, he allows, must be loosely constructed, e.g. the novel. Again, some music lacks the quality of unity, although such music he insists we do not call fine music.

I want to by-pass the obvious point that the sense of the term unity is so vague as to preclude reasonable debate about the application of the term to the various arts. Rather, I want to ask whether there are not paintings which we can call works of art and which do not meet Osborne's requirement. It is patent that there are forms of art, Persian and Oriental, in which a portion of the work, a part of a screen, a top of a miniature may be removed without altering the quality of the work. It is also obvious that there is a whole school of contemporary painting, e.g. abstract painting, which does not in some instances depict anything, and in other cases does not seek to create three-dimensional space.

Why then does Osborne insist that we *must* actualize the aesthetic object in the way he describes? What is the force of the must? The answer that unless we do so we shall not have an aesthetic object to contemplate is trivial, since this is just how Osborne defines aesthetic object. That such an object is the fittest object for aesthetic contemplation does not carry us further if aesthetic contemplation is simply the contemplation of aesthetic objects. The justification of the definition travels in a circle, and the definition, by Osborne's own admission applies, if it applies at all, to a small number of works of art. It is a pity that Osborne chose for his model a form of art, easel painting, which has flourished most in the 19th century, and many of whose features are not at all representative of what is present in other art forms. But even so, Osborne's claim seems inapplicable in the very area he chooses for the support of his position. Part of this is obscured by Osborne's talk of seeing both the detail and the general features. In a depicted scene a fold in a silk dress may be a detail, and the relation of the figures on the scene a general feature, but a brush stroke is not a detail of which the organization of *figures* in the scene is a general feature, a brush stroke is a detail in a series of brush strokes. The character of the brush strokes, say, short, then, overlapping, and so on, may very well give a quality to the painting, but the brush strokes are not details of which the quality of the painting is a feature.

My point, more generally is that what Osborne is demanding is impossible and the impossibility is obscured by characterizing a painter's technique as a detail of the painting. Osborne, to repeat, requires us to see the picture simultaneously as a textured surface, as a configuration of flat patterns, and as a deep three-dimensional pattern. I suggest that this can't be done and that if it could be done the three elements would not necessarily be seen as belonging together. We can pay attention to the design and then our sense of the depiction fades into the background. It is not the center of our attention. We can look carefully at the strokes, but then organization and depiction are no longer what we can pay attention to. You cannot both try to listen to a man's argument and pay attention to the sound of his speech or his patterns of intonation, and give them equal attention.

Osborne is aware of this criticism and he tries to handle it in two ways. He first concedes that what he is describing is *logically* impossible! Seeing something as pattern and as representation "are both legitimate and necessary ways of seeing which though logically incompatible combine with mutual enrichment" (p. 181). "These logical contradictions," he writes "do not in fact apply in perception" (p. 180). I should have thought that the logically impossible entails the physically impossible. In any event Osborne does not produce any example of self-contradictory statements. To say that I see the picture simultaneously as a textured surface and as a depiction is not to utter two *logically* incompatible utterances at all.

Osborne's claim is that aesthetic perception is "a mode of percipience which excludes conceptualization" hence its results are not entirely amenable to conceptual description. This is a pretty obvious nonsequitur; moreover, Osborne claims to describe the results. What he can't explain is how results which are admitted to be impossible are achieved. He concedes the claim of the Gestalt psychologists that in perception the figure-ground principle holds. "We look at a painting as *representational* in accordance with the same principles of perception as we employ in ordinary life" (p. 195). But we must simultaneously see it this way, and as a configuration of prescribed forms. Now it turns out that *two* "modes of percipience" must operate at once!

Osborne is led to his claim of a "nonconceptual mode of percipience" it seems to me, because he holds, first of all, that the aesthetic object must be a "configurational unity" and that the object is organized and apprehended by us. That it should be the former does not entail that the latter should hold. Osborne himself concedes that what he is demanding is impossible in the case of music. "It is no doubt impossible to perform a Beethoven Sonata in such a way as to give ideal expression at once to the melodic line, to the contrapuntal intricacies, and to the dramatic force . . . our conception of the work of art is . . . a composite concept taking in both the performances we have enjoyed and our own ideas of how these performances fell short of perfection and the insights which each revealed" (p. 187). Thus at the outset the demand which he makes for pictures, he abandons for music. Aesthetic percipience is now not the only mode of contemplating works of art. Our only question now is whether any such mode exists at all.

My claim is that we have no reason for thinking anything of the sort

Osborne describes exists. There is no empirical evidence which supports the claim, since what aesthetic percipience is supposed to perform cannot be performed. But if it did exist, its value would be quite circumscribed. The claim that a work was *not* unified would have to be discovered and made by what Osborne calls our practical or discursive faculty of apprehension. All our perceptions of inferior works now apparently pose no difficulty for conceptualization.

Osborne's claim is this: when "we become aware of two or more pattern-groups related to each other but not assimilated into a higher embracing configuration, we build up knowledge discursively, about them" (p. 187). Thus, presumably when I look at three paintings which are in a row on a wall, my knowledge that there are three paintings in rectangular frames and so on is discursive because what I observe is not a unity. Osborne is talking, here, of *knowledge* built up discursively, rather than perception, but if we ignore this, we can take him as claiming that when what we perceive "is a plurality of configurations standing only in external relations" our apprehension of the object is theoretical or discursive. When the configurations are perceived as elements in a high-level configuration our apprehension is aesthetic (p. 187). There is an odd asymmetry here. When what we perceive is externally related there is no suggestion that its properties are the work of the perceiver. But the aesthetic properties are the work of aesthetic percipience, and what it is about the work which makes it amenable to this sort of operation remains a mystery. It would be singular to offer this thesis to the practicing artist. It is not clear how he would know whether he was producing a work of art.

It is a further oddity of Osborne's aesthetic faculty that while it is nonconceptual, it must operate in some cooperation with cognitive faculties — that is, we must understand the words of a novel; we must know what is depicted in the painting, and know also the meaning of whatever symbols are in it. Osborne's way out is to suggest that these are nonaesthetic features. But this simply equates "aesthetic" with "nondiscursive" and is at odds with his claim that what he says applies in principle to our enjoyment of the beauty and elegance of a mathematical theorem or chess problem.

There is a final reason one can find in Osborne for his belief that aesthetic apprehension, though a cognitive activity, cannot be itself characterized. It is the claim that aesthetic qualities are unrepeatable and hence not characterizable. Both claims seem to me false. Aesthetic qualities are repeatable. We can play the same record twice, a fact acknowledged by Osborne in allowing that after a given time we may tire of a work. And second, an extraordinary variety of qualities and shapes is still amenable to some classification. We are told that no human beings have identical fingerprints, but this has not prevented the creation of a workable system for classifying them.

We can return now to our first question. What is the nature of the art of appreciation, the skill which presumably it was Osborne's purpose to describe? The answer now seems to be that it is not describable. The aesthetic activity is not amenable to analysis. Thus the skill competent observers practice is a skill which cannot be taught. I have suggested also that it is a skill which as Osborne describes it is impossible to perform. We are left not to ask why anyone should wish to practice it.

Osborne, we may recall, maintains that any object may be the object of aesthetic attention (p. 31). It is a fixing of attention upon a presented object and a process of bringing ourselves to awareness of that object in perception (p. 31). It is also a state of calm, of arrest (p. 30). It is a form of contemplation which excludes "theorizing about the object," i.e. classifying it, thinking of its causal relations, and so on. Yet most objects are incapable of sustaining aesthetic contemplation for long. A work of art is an object which when contemplated aesthetically results in an aesthetic object. An aesthetic object is an entity whose parts form a complex unity. Its merit as an aesthetic object is that it provides an object for aesthetic contemplation. Aesthetic contemplation is the art of regarding or holding the parts of an aesthetic object together as parts of a unity. Aesthetic enjoyment is the enjoyment of the skill of contemplating aesthetic objects.

I should have thought that what one enjoyed was the aesthetic object, or at least that the contemplation of the object was enjoyable. If what one enjoyed was one's skill in contemplating—if that makes sense at all—then one would not be enjoying aesthetic objects but the skill that produced them. One can enjoy eating pies, or enjoy making them. But they are distinct enough so that one could enjoy the latter without enjoying the former, and in aesthetics this would be odd, indeed.

If, moreover, what we are after is a prolongation of aesthetic perception then it would be an empirical matter whether this sort of perception was prolonged by an object of one sort rather than another. There would be nothing wrong in claiming that a given object would prolong aesthetic contemplation although the object was not a complex unity of the sort required.

In fact aesthetic percipience is now defined as precisely the skill of apprehending such complex unities. But it would follow, I think, that the claim that any object might be the object of aesthetic percipience would be false. The delight in the color of a leaf, or the circle made by birds in the sky could no longer be called aesthetic. But if one makes the activity primary, objects are aesthetic only by courtesy. It would follow too that it was only a contingent matter that works of art had anything to do with aesthetic contemplation.

And I think too that one would be hard pressed, not merely to justify the place of the arts in society, but art itself. Osborne is so afraid of using the term "pleasure" at all in connection with art — he writes with contempt of sordid hedonism — that the delight and enjoyment which attend our interaction with works of art are hardly touched on.

But apart from this, it seems to me that the justification of aesthetics moves in a circle. Aesthetic perception is justified because it results in aesthetic objects whose merit is that they are objects for the exercise of aesthetic perception. Or if it is defined as a nondiscursive awareness of complex unities, one's first question here is why should anyone regard this as valuable. Osborne has so cut himself off from the kinds of things that one says of art, both in its praise and defense, that one cannot find a way to make clear what many of us find in art that makes us value it. And this I think, is the most effective criticism to offer of his definition of aesthetics.

The Omnicolored Sky: Baylis
on Perception

John Lachs
Vanderbilt University

Baylis's published work contains the outlines of a theory of perception. He never developed the view in the detail it deserves and needs for a full defense. His students report that his lectures contained elaborations of the theory beyond anything he committed to print. Unfortunately, however, I have no reliable access to these lectures. I must base my reflections on what he has published so far and for the rest content myself with the hope that he will soon publish more.

What is available by Baylis on perception shares the crispness, clarity and charm of his other published work. In these essays, as elsewhere, he shows himself as an honest, serious and level-headed thinker. He has a respect for the facts of experience which rivals that of the most devoted phenomenologist. He is keenly aware of the social or cooperative nature of philosophy: his own ideas are developed with constant reference to what others have thought and he is glad to rely on whatever advances Price, Broad, Lewis or Chisholm may have made.

There are at least two reasons why his theory of perception was never systematically developed. The first is this very reliance on the work of others. He obviously feels that many important topics have been discussed well enough by others; there is no need for him to duplicate their work. The second is that much of his writing in this area has polemical objectives. He launches repeated attacks on epistemological dualism, especially as it is found in Lovejoy's work. His longest article in the field is a critical study of Chisholm's *Perceiving.*[1] Another long and interesting piece is largely reportive.[2] Even in his most recent paper on the subject, which bears the promising title "Foundations for a Presentative Theory

---

1. C. A. Baylis, "Professor Chisholm on Perceiving," *The Journal of Philosophy,* 56 (1959), 773–791.
2. C. A. Baylis, "The Given and Perceptual Knowledge," In *Philosophic Thought in France and the United States,* ed. Marvin Farber (Buffalo, 1950). Referred to as "Given" hereafter.

of Perception and Sensation,"[3] he cannot resist the temptation to devote a few pages to attacking Lovejoy.

In terminology that undergoes some changes from article to article, Baylis maintains as his main thesis that for the most part we perceive physical objects "correctly and directly."[4] That physical objects exist independently of perceptions and perceivers and that veridical perception of them is possible are minimal tenets of realism. I accept them in philosophy as I accept them in daily life. To do otherwise would make philosophy contrived or an irrelevant intellectual exercise. This will immediately identify my disagreements with Baylis as a family quarrel. Both of us believe in the independent existence of the physical world and both of us look to science for more information about the process that underlies perception. But family squabbles are notoriously vehement, even though it is often difficult to tell what precisely separates the parties.

How very difficult it is to identify the difference between Baylis and the critical realists he so vigorously attacks is best seen by examining what he calls the "basic theses" of his "epistemological monism."[5] Baylis notes nine such theses. The first three are simply an expanded statement of realism: the critical realist embraces them as readily as the "epistemological monist." They are:

(1) There is a real world of objects and events which exists independently of our knowledge of them.
(2) We can and often do perceive such objects and events.
(3) In the vast majority of cases we perceive them veridically, although of course this does not mean that we perceive everything about any of them.[6]

The next proposition Baylis wishes to affirm is completely innocuous. To say that

(4) Where we misperceive we can learn of our errors and their sources from scientists who study perception by attending to objects and events and people's reports about their experiences of such objects and events

is not to assert anything controversial. Even a man of Berkeley's persuasion could subscribe to this view. And a proposition that is inadequate

3. *Proceedings of the Aristotelian Society,* ns, 66 (1965–66), 41–54. Referred to as "Foundations" hereafter.
4. "Foundations," 41.
5. C. A. Baylis, "A Criticism of Lovejoy's Case for Epistemological Dualism," *Philosophy and Phenomenological Research,* 23 (1962–63), 536. Referred to as "Criticism" hereafter.
6. "Criticism," 536.

to distinguish between idealists and realists can surely not be what differentiates one realist from another.

(5) Sense-data can be observed when we are sensibly stimulated, but need not be and usually are not. They are of most use for artists, beauty-lovers, and psychologists and of very little use for perceptual knowledge.

(6) Sense-data are usually coincident with the surfaces of objects.

Here Baylis's position appears commonsensical. He believes that for the most part when we believe that we perceive a physical object, we do in fact perceive one. In such cases typically we do not observe sense data, sensible qualities[7] or *qualia*.[8] Such sensible qualities are, however, probably always involved in our perception and we tend to be "sensibly aware"[9] of them when they are striking or unusual. Thus on seeing the victim of an automobile accident, we may note the pallor of his face. Or if we could touch Cleopatra's hand, we may well note with surprise that it is broken out.

Now these seem to me to be altogether harmless distinctions. There is no reason why a critical realist could not embrace them. One could, of course, say a number of things about sense-data, even in the sense in which Baylis uses the term, which would help to distinguish one sort of realist from another. But Baylis emphatically steers clear of any such. He says little about the precise relation of sensible qualities to physical objects and nothing of the role *qualia* play in perception or the recognition of objects. He does not discuss the ontological status of sense-data and the apparent particulars of immediate experience which he calls "sensa."[10] And he simply sidesteps the problem of the relation of such sensa to full-bodied physical objects.

Even the claim of (6) is too weak to be of value here. The "coincidence" of a sense-datum with the surface of a physical object leaves it possible for datum and surface to be numerically distinct. The slip cover designed to look exactly like the seat it hides is coincident without being identical with it. The epistemological monist must insist on the identity and it is puzzling, to say the least, why Baylis does not.

The next two propositions are also perfectly acceptable to critical realists. (7) is a natural corollary of a realist and causal theory of perception, while (8) follows from (1) and (2).

---

7. "Foundations," 47.
8. "Given," 451.
9. "Foundations," 47.
10. "Given," 451.

(7) Images, on the other hand, are bits of mental content which have been internally, not externally, aroused. They are the stuff of hallucinations.

(8) The objects that one person perceives are often perceived and are almost always perceivable by others. They are public constituents of our common world.

This leaves us with (9) as the only proposition by which to distinguish Baylis's view from the realism he criticizes.

(9) Perception is usually *direct,* not in the sense of having no necessary means but in the sense of not involving conscious inference.

Baylis evidently considers the idea of the directness of perception very important. He returns to it again and again and in each case he makes clear that by "direct" he means "without conscious inference."[11] And, if this is what it means to perceive directly, Baylis is entirely right. Of course there is no psychological sequence of receiving data, organizing them and then consciously inferring the existence of external objects. The philosopher who held this view of simple perception, if indeed anyone ever held it, should no more be debated than the man who believes that a heap of cinderblocks is an amorous princess. He should be told to go look again and not to return until he learns to rule his fancy.

Why Baylis should suppose that critical realists are committed to belief in a *conscious inference* from datum to object I simply do not know. He is aware that the dualists he wishes to attack insist on the numerical (though not on the qualitative) diversity of what is immediately present in consciousness and the physical object we perceive. The datum, therefore, is in some way intermediary in perception: it is only by means of it, by utilizing it somehow that we can perceive the independently existing material world. Perhaps Baylis thinks that the necessary mediation can only take the form of inference. But there is little reason to suppose that data are used as premises and none at all that that is the only way they can be used. There is no conscious inference even in the case of such simple sign-relations as my thinking that it will rain on seeing gray-black clouds. And in reading we surely make no inference, conscious or unconscious, from printed shapes to meanings. We deal there with a noninferential mediation, the sort that is typical of symbols. The same or almost the same is true of situations in which a casual gesture signifies rejection or a Rohrschach blot is seen as an obscene scene.

I will not deny that if we were asked for a justification of what we think or see or understand in the above cases, we would attempt to infer the

11. "Foundations," 42, 47.

desired conclusions from some reasonably acceptable premises. But it would be a mistake to confuse the structure of justification with the processes of consciousness. I also admit that the critical realist's idea of the way in which the sensibly given stands for external objects needs to be developed in detail. Along with every other known philosophical theory, it suffers from difficulties and has to meet a variety of objections. But my present task is not that of elaborating and defending this view. I simply wish to establish that critical realism does not commit one to maintaining that there is a conscious inference from datum to physical object. It is far more plausible, in fact, to construe the relation of what is immediately present to what is perceived on the analogy or as a type of symbolic designation. At least one part of the reason for this is that viewing the datum as symbol does not go blatantly against the facts of experience. Viewing it as premise for inference in simple cases of perception clearly does. Baylis does not seem to realize that no critical realist need be committed to the thesis that conscious inferences are inextricably involved in perception. As a result, he fails to consider alternative, and more plausible, critical realist accounts of the relation of datum to physical object. Even more distressingly, as I trust my argument so far has shown, he simply does not succeed in distinguishing his own brand of realism from the dualistic one.

This appears to me particularly surprising, since the distinction is readily at hand. Whatever else critical realists maintain, they insist on the numerical diversity of datum and physical object. Direct realists deny this, either because they think there is no special (for instance, private) given element in perception or because they feel confident that the given is actually a constituent of the physical object. Critical realists must explain how the datum can yield knowledge of the object. Direct realists face the opposite problem of how we can ever err if our contact with the object is immediate.

The initial tendency of the critical realist is to say that the datum and the physical object simply *cannot* be identical. There is a powerful spatial image behind this conviction. The object, we think, is *out there*. It sends reports of itself into my head, where the process or act of perception or at least the processes necessary for perception occur. What is present in the brain can surely not be numerically one with what is at a distance from it and was its partial cause. This captivating picture is reinforced by what we know of the physical and physiological conditions of perception. In reflecting on these it is brought home to us that the separation of the immediately presented from the presumably unpresented but perceived object is temporal as well as spatial. In the case of distant stars the temporal lag may be so great that by the time their light reaches us they no longer exist.

But neither this image nor these reflections suffice to show that direct realism is an absurd or blatantly false view. Baylis is entirely correct in arguing against Lovejoy that we must distinguish the processes of perception from its objects.[12] And if this distinction is made, Baylis can readily accept all the mediating organs and processes scientists will ever find, without having to yield the claim of direct cognitive contact. For, he argues, the spatio-temporal separation is between the act or process of perceiving and the object perceived.[13] The processes of perception are physical and mediated. At about the time of the last event of the physiological portion of these processes an epistemological relation arises between the perceiver and the object that stimulated him. Even though the physical process is mediated, there is no requirement that the cognitive relation it makes possible shall share this property. What makes the critical realist position appear plausible here is the supposition that in addition to processes there are also some data or objects in the brain. That, however, is just a way of assuming what was to be proved, viz. the critical realist view of the duality of data and what they reveal.

This argument successfully shows that Baylis's view is entirely possible. But is it at all plausible? The first remark to make is that Baylis deftly sidesteps the difficult issue of accounting for perceptual error. He does this by simply not distinguishing between the question of what causes perceptual error and the analysis of what such error consists in. There is little doubt that misperception occurs as a result of something going wrong in the process or medium or organs involved.[14] But to say that fire is caused by striking matches is not to give an account of what it is. Similarly, to identify the sources of perceptual error is not to explain its nature.

Actually, if Baylis had undertaken the task of dealing with the problem of error in earnest, he would have found it to be even more difficult than the previous comment suggests. He would have had to explain not only what error is but also how it is possible if his view is correct. Let us accept, for a moment, the claim that in perception we stand in direct cognitive relation to the surfaces of physical objects. Viewed internally, viz. from the standpoint of the experience itself, perceptions and misperceptions are notoriously indistinguishable. Among other similarities, each has a qualitied thing, event or fact as its object. How could Baylis draw the line between veridical perceptions, misperceptions and hallucinations?

He appears to have four alternatives. (1) He could maintain that each putative case of perception is veridical. But this is clearly unacceptable

12. "Criticism," 530.
13. Ibid., 531.
14. Ibid., 534.

and would signal the bankruptcy of his view. (2) He could modify this claim and hold that although each putative case of perception is veridical as and when undergone, we judge some to be erroneous in the light of other and for the most part later experiences. But this blurs the important distinction between the erroneousness of perceptions and the way in which this is determined. In addition, it is seriously at odds with Baylis's realistic idea that there are "hard," determinate, mind-independent facts.[15] If some of these at least can be perceived, they can also be misperceived, and that independently of what we judge of the matter later. (3) He could admit the distinction between perception and misperception and characterize the latter as consisting of (a) direct perceptual contact with the object and (b) perceptual acceptance of the object as exemplifying qualities or relations it does not possess. But this does not account for hallucinations. In addition, since the percipient is immediately acquainted with the quality that by (b) does not characterize the object, Baylis must concede a duality of datum and the qualities of the object in at least some cases. This occasional failure of identity, combined with the internal indistinguishability of perceptions and misperceptions, can now be used by the critical realist to cast doubt on the numerical identity of experienced and embodied characters in any case. And if the general duality of presented and embodied characters is admitted, the thesis of direct contact with the object becomes untenable. (4) He could maintain that in veridical perception we are in direct cognitive contact with the object, but in misperceptions and hallucinations we are not. But this is an even easier target for the critical realist than (3). For here in all but veridical cases we have an admitted duality of datum and object. Given the internal indistinguishability of the cases it is then extremely difficult to make selective identity plausible.

It is possible that Baylis may come up with some other, perhaps novel and surprising account of the nature and possibility of perceptual error. Until he does, however, I shall move on to another matter.

Baylis maintains that when there is nothing "odd"[16] in the psychophysiological process of perception, about the time of the last event of this process a cognitive relationship emerges. This relation is a direct and probably unique one between the percipient and the physical object that initiated the process. The characteristic claim of presentative realism is that the object in perceptual consciousness *is* the physical object: there is no immanent object of awareness by means of which the transcendent object is cognized. This simple view seems at first blush very attractive. But it has some very strange consequences.

15. C. A. Baylis, "Facts, Propositions, Exemplification and Truth," *Mind*, ns, 57 (1948), 459ff.
16. "Criticism," 534.

Suppose we perceive a distant star that, in the time it took for its light to reach our eyes, has ceased to exist. If what is present to consciousness is the star itself, then the star still exists. Again, if the star is identical with what is present to us and it is no more, we can have nothing present to consciousness. To say that we perceive the star as it *was*[17] seems little more than a verbal gloss. If what is present now is literally identical with the surface of the star, that heavenly body cannot be nonexistent. And, conversely, if the star is nonexistent, we cannot be in contact with its surface. This result can be generalized to apply to all cases of perception. Since the perceptual process invariably takes time, what we perceive on Baylis's view is always the object "as and where it . . . was"[18] at the time of the initiation of the process. In what sense can the currently observed state of an object be identical with a hitherto unobserved past state of it? There can, of course, be qualitative identity: the two can exhibit identical qualities and relations. But this is not the sort of identity Baylis seeks. And to get anything stronger we would have to treat each surface as a quasi-substance that endures retaining its identity through change and time.

There may, however, be another line Baylis can take at this point. He could redefine the boundaries of the object in such a way that a very large number of diverse sensa could all be legitimately considered as constituents of it. Some of these constituents could well linger on long after the nuclear members of the collection that is the thing have ceased to exist.[19] If he held some such view, Baylis could maintain that what we perceive is very frequently or almost always the physical thing itself. For then the physical object would, in effect, consist only or largely of such perceived or perceptible sensa.

Such an account of the architecture of the thing is not easily compatible with commonsense realism. Moreoever, Baylis neither considers nor adopts this view. But he does discuss Price's ideas, which make in this direction, in a complimentary fashion.[20] And he himself comes close to such a wide, if not loose, definition of the constituents of physical objects in what he says about their color *qualia*. It is to this issue that I now turn.

At first sight, Baylis's view of the color of objects is a fascinating mix of the charmingly simple and the infuriating. Any object, he says, "has all the colours it is . . . reported to have."[21] Thus, it seems, the sky is truly blue if it is perceived as manifesting that color. But it is also grey,

17. Ibid., 531.
18. Ibid.
19. I use "nuclear members" in the sense Price gives the phrase. See H. H. Price, *Perception* (London, 1954), p. 222.
20. "Given," 454ff.
21. "Foundations," 53.

yellow, purple and middle brown, if it is honestly reported to have those colors. Baylis even goes a step further. Physical objects have not only the colors they are actually observed as having. They are characterized by every one of the color qualities they *could* be seen to display, if only lighting conditions and perceivers with the requisite (or requisitely strange) perceptual faculties were at hand.[22] And supposedly they are characterized by these vast numbers of colors simultaneously.

It is a generally accepted and hence infrequently uttered claim among painters, philosophers and interior decorators, at least, that two colors cannot suffuse the same surface at the same time. Different observers may, of course, see the sky or a yard of cloth as of different colors, as may the same observer at different times. But this is not what Baylis has in mind. He seems to think that the sky *is in fact* characterized by all those colors, though it takes a different set of lighting conditions and a special sort of eyes to detect each. Surely, the principle of the incompatibility of colors could not have escaped as acute a logician as Baylis. One's first inclination, therefore, is to interpret this view as amounting to a bold challenge of that principle.

If this should propel one to examine the literature, one will soon find that very few reasons have ever been offered, and perhaps none should be accepted, for the supposition that two determinates of the same determinable cannot characterize a given item. For that matter, I cannot recall any reason other than the general nominalist conviction that determinables should be run back to their determinates, that has ever been offered against the mad metaphysical possibility that determinables may be embodied without the concurrent embodiment of any of their determinates. One could spend interesting hours speculating on these matters, but it seems to me that in the current context this would be pointless. The reason is twofold. First of all, to embrace such a counterintuitive thesis as the compatibility of determinates is sheer bravado. A view of perception that implies or requires it is so much the worse off. Even if it could be shown that no contradiction is involved, the implausibility of the compatibility thesis is so great that it cannot but carry over to the view that implies it. Secondly, it is not at all clear to what Baylis's claim of omnicolored objects actually amounts. There is, I want to argue, good reason to doubt (1) that his position commits him to omnicolored objects in the onerous sense, (2) that he has adequate reason for saying that objects are omnicolored in that sense, and (3) that when he says that objects are omnicolored he does so in full and clear consciousness of the alternatives and consequences.

Let me put my cards directly on the table. It seems to me that Baylis speaks of color in three different and inadequately distinguished ways. He

22. "Criticism," 534.

begins by talking of color as a sensory property or power.[23] As such, any object has exactly as many "colors" as there are different color experiences it can evoke. There is nothing mysterious about this, nor anything objectionable. If the colors of things are merely the powers they have to cause specific sorts of sensations, each object can be, in fact probably is, omnicolored without incompatibility.

Now when "colors" in the sense of dispositions or sensory properties are brought in the proper conjunction with beings endowed with the requisite sense organs, they give rise to experienced colors. In the current sense, "colors" are sensible qualities of which we are conscious and which usually appear to characterize physical objects. On this view color is relational. Though from the standpoint of direct experience colors are simple qualities, their apparent inherence in objects is the result of a relation. No object can, then, be said to be of any color in and of itself. It will have the color C on condition that it has the sensory property x, that the intervening medium is in state y and that a percipient with sense organs of type z is present. A change in any of these conditions will involve a change in color or a change from perceiving an object as colored to perceiving nothing at all. Once again, objects can be — and probably are — omnicolored in this sense without any incompatibility.

What puzzles me is the move Baylis makes at this point. He notes that "different people or the same people in different circumstances report"[24] that a given object has many different colors. "Why not say," he boldly asks, "that its surface has all . . . [of these] color qualities. . . ."[25] This seems to be a perfectly acceptable way of speaking, so long as we remember that the object has these color qualities relationally. But here Baylis takes or appears to take a giant step. He continues the sentence I just quoted as follows: ". . . its surface has all . . . [of these] color qualities, though for these to be seen requires special combinations of a light ray of a certain sort with a perceiver of a certain sort."

Here it no longer seems that the colors of objects are relational. Colors seem to inhere in objects as primaries, quite independently of whether there is anyone there to perceive them. Special lighting conditions and special sorts of eyes give us access to these objectively inherent colors. When red light is shed on a go-go dancer's body, this reveals to us a color that has been there all along, instead of being one of the conditions without which the color would not exist.

This position seems to me excessively improbable. That objects are omnicolored in this sense does not follow from the fact that they are omnicolored in the other two senses I have distinguished. And such a

23. "Foundations," 48.
24. "Criticism," 534.
25. Ibid.

view is, of course, not readily harmonized with commonsense or the findings of science. Baylis could, here again, maintain that the object is but a large collection of sensa: this would leave ample room for every color quality to be a constituent of it. But, as I suggested earlier, this view itself is difficult to reconcile with Baylis's commonsense realism.

Does Baylis really mean to hold the idea that things in the world are objectively omnicolored? The passages I quoted, from one of the two articles where he discusses the matter, suggest that he does. Yet there is room for doubt. Consider these statements from the other of the two papers.

> Suppose the lighting conditions, X, remain constant throughout. Why not assume that the object has the power or capacity or dispositional property under these conditions to cause all those with a-type eyes to see colour 1? Similarly, it has the power to cause all those with b-type eyes to see colour 2. Again it has the power or capacity to cause all those with c-type eyes to see colour 3. Why not assume that the object has *in this sense*, at least, all these colours, since it has all these powers?[26]

Objects are indeed omnicolored "in this sense": they do indeed have the power to cause different color-perceptions in different perceivers. An even more pointed statement comes from a letter to the author.

> And there is no need to insist on just one real color per surface. Why not say that every surface has all the colors it can be seen to have under all possible combinations of the variable conditions required? A is red under conditions abd . . . gray under conditions ayc, blue under conditions acx, etc. etc. *To say that it is that color under those conditions is to say that the specified color will be seen under those conditions.*[27]

If he thinks that to say that a given object is a certain color is to say no more than that under specifiable conditions that color will be seen to suffuse it, Baylis is clearly not committed to objectively inherent colors. Yet immediately following the passage from "Foundations for a Presentative Theory of Perception and Sensation" I quoted above, he says, "Different people simply have different powers to discern the different colors the object exhibits." To *discern* the colors of objects is a very different matter from experiencing objects as characterized by colors that vary with the conditions of perception. Whether these apparent differences in what Baylis maintains are due simply to careless phrasing, I cannot decide.

26. "Foundations," 53, my italics.
27. Letter to the author, dated April 11, 1966, my italics.

Is Baylis's presentative realism defensible? A full defense of it would presuppose its full development. But Baylis's position is neither fully developed nor unambiguous. For this reason, one can only guess at how probable it could be made and how its strengths and weaknesses would compare with those of rival theories. The fact that he starts from a realistic premise inclines me to think that he is near the truth. But the difficulties inherent in the idea that we are in direct cognitive contact with the physical world make me suspect that he is not near enough.

Causation in Perception

P. F. Strawson
Oxford University

For any given description or specification of what I shall call a material object array (M-array) we can distinguish between three conditions: (1) perceiving such an array (e.g. seeing a book on a desk in front of you, or hearing an aeroplane flying overhead); (2) believing or taking it that you perceive such an array; (3) its sensibly seeming to you just as if you perceive such an array. These conditions are logically independent of each other in that, for a given specification of a material object array, any one of the three conditions can be satisfied without either of the other two being satisfied and any two can be satisfied without the third being satisfied. For example, think of a case in which you are looking at what you know very well to be a solid object — say a bush — standing in front of a wall; but for a moment it looks to you just like, you *see it as,* something drawn on the surface of the wall. Then, for one specification of an M-array, we have the first two conditions satisfied without the third; and for another specification we have the third condition satisfied without the other two.

I shall refer to these three conditions by the use of the following abbreviations: (1) M-perception; (2) M-perception-belief; (3) M-perception-experience (or M-experience).

Here is one familiar entailment. If you are having a certain M-perception, then a corresponding M-array exists or corresponding or appropriate M-facts obtain. (If you see a book on a desk in front of you, then there is a book on a desk in front of you.) I shall write this as:

I   (1) → appropriate M-facts.

Of course no such entailment holds with regard to either of the other two conditions.

A certain relation weaker than entailment holds in one direction, though not in the other, between condition (3) and each of the other two conditions — for any given specification of an M-array. *Normally* or *generally,* when condition (3) is satisfied for a given M-array specification, condition (2) is satisfied as well. To put it colloquially, we normally believe, e.g., our own eyes or, in general, what our senses seem to tell us. Again, when condition (3) is satisfied for a given M-array specification, condition (1) is normally satisfied as well. (The point indeed might be held to be implicit in the description of condition (3).) Colloquially, we are normally right in believing, e.g., our own eyes. We may call this weaker relation than entailment that of *presumptive implication;* and write it as follows:

II   (3) o→ (1)
III   (3) o→ (2).

This relation by no means holds in the other direction. For there are countless true specifications or descriptions of the things we, e.g., *see* — and countless such descriptions which we believe to be true — which do not, and perhaps could not — figure in any truthful account of, e.g., how those things *look* to us. Examples would be the descriptions 'married five times', as applied to a man, or 'once shaken by the Queen', as applied to a hand. So we do not have: (1) o→ (3); and we do not have: (2) o→ (3).

The relations I have mentioned have certain further consequences. Thus from I and II there follows

IV   (3) o→ appropriate M-facts.

If, for any M-array specification, it is normally the case that if (3) then (1), and if (1) entails appropriate M-facts, then it is normally the case that if (3), then appropriate M-facts.

To this we can add

V   (3) o→ belief in appropriate M-facts.

V holds as a direct consequence of III alone. For, as I am using the expressions, we should not count anyone as believing that he was having a certain M-perception unless he believed that appropriate M-facts obtained.

There is something else we can add. We can say that the fact that relation II holds makes it *normally reasonable* to hold the belief referred to at III; and correspondingly the fact that relation IV holds makes it *normally reasonable* to hold the belief referred to at V. That is to say, we can read the ring-and-arrow of III and V in two ways: both as, originally, 'presumptively implies' and as 'presumptively makes reasonable'. One might express the point by saying that normally an M-experience carries a *belief-title* with it, a title to be taken to be the M-perception it seems to be; and consequently that it carries with it a title to belief in appropriate or corresponding M-facts. This is not to say, of course, that the title cannot be challenged, only that it *needs* to be: that there has to be some special reason for not taking the M-experience to be the M-perception it seems to be, for not taking it that appropriate M-facts obtain.

Now if one is having an M-experience and if corresponding M-facts obtain, does it follow that one is having the corresponding M-perception? That is to say, does the following hold (for a given M-array specification):

(3) + appropriate M-facts → (1)?

For example, if it sensibly seems to one just as if one were seeing a book on a desk in front of one and if there is in front of one just such a book on just such a desk as it sensibly seems to one as if one were seeing, does it follow that one is seeing the book on the desk in front of one?

Professor Grice has argued convincingly, indeed conclusively, that it does not follow.[1] He makes, and illustrates, the point that it is logically possible that the M-perception-experience should have been produced by unusual methods—e.g. cortical stimulation, suggestion, an arrangement of mirrors and objects—methods which could have been used to produce the M-experience even if there had been no appropriate M-facts. He concludes that for an M-experience to be the M-perception it seems to be, it is necessary not only that the appropriate M-facts should obtain, but also that the M-experience should be causally dependent on those M-facts.

This is not to report him quite exactly. He draws in fact a more general conclusion of which that just reported is a consequence and to which I shall refer later. But let us for the moment consider the restricted conclusion. It would be generally agreed to be a logically necessary condition of an M-experience being the M-perception it seems to be, that appropriate M-facts should obtain. What we are now confronted with is the thought that it is also a logically necessary condition of the M-experience being the M-perception it seems to be, that the obtaining of the appropriate M-facts should be a causally, or nonlogically, necessary condition of the occurrence of the M-experience.

Let us accept this conclusion—indeed I think we *have* to accept it—and inquire into its *rationale,* the way it fits in to our general concept of perception.

Let us begin by noting another of those presumptive relations, weaker than entailment, which I have been setting out. There is absolutely no need to appeal to any specialist or scientific considerations in order to make the following point; viz. that our M-experience *normally* or *generally is* nonlogically or causally dependent on appropriate M-facts. All we need to do to establish the point is to appeal to such familiar facts as this: that if it sensibly seems to one just as if one were seeing a pencil held before one's eyes, then not only is it normally the case that there is a

1. See "The Causal Theory of Perception," *Proceedings of the Aristotelian Society,* sup. vol. (1961).

pencil held before one's eyes, it is also normally the case that if the pencil is, say, taken away and held behind the holder's back, one will no longer seem to see it, i.e. no longer have the M-experience in question. It is beyond dispute that such a fact typifies the general or normal character of our perceptual experience. That I correctly count what subjectively happens as seeing a pencil held before my eyes depends in every case, logically, on there being a pencil held before my eyes; but that there subjectively happens that which I *normally* count (correctly or not) as seeing a pencil held before my eyes *normally* depends, nonlogically or causally, on there being a pencil held before my eyes.

I have just said that such a fact typifies the general or normal character of our perceptual experience. Of course the thesis of the general or normal causal dependence of M-experiences on appropriate M-facts must be acknowledged to differ in certain respects from many theses of causal dependence. It is not established by noting correlations between independently observable states of affairs. For one cannot *observe* that M-facts appropriate to certain M-experiences obtain without there occurring just such experiences as are in question. Thereby, no doubt, hangs many a tale. But this difference is not such as to *weaken* the general thesis. It serves, rather, to explain why the general thesis is one of those truths which are so obvious that they are easy to overlook.

In addition, then, to the weak relations already noted, we have the following:

VI   (3) o→ the M-experience is causally dependent on appropriate M-facts.

Note that VI entails a fortiori the truth we have already numbered IV, i.e. (3) o→ appropriate M-facts.

But now what of the relations between proposition VI – the presumptive relation resting on the fact that M-experiences are normally causally dependent on appropriate M-facts – and the proposition we seem bound to accept, viz. that a particular M-experience is the M-perception it seems to be only if, besides appropriate M-facts obtaining, that particular M-experience is causally dependent on those M-facts? This proposition is not entailed by proposition VI, nor by the conjunction of proposition VI and proposition I, nor by any other combination of the already established relations. It has yet to be shown that there is a rational connexion between these relations and the proposition we seem bound to accept. It can be shown, perhaps, as follows.

The association between M-experiences and appropriate M-facts, though normal, is not, of course, invariable. An M-experience may occur without appropriate M-facts obtaining. Then we may say that it is, in part or wholly, an *illusory* M-experience. Now if an M-experience occurs without appropriate M-facts obtaining, it follows, of course, at once, that the causes of that M-experience, whatever they may be, do not include the obtaining of appropriate M-facts. So we have to recognize the existence of a class of M-experiences of which the causes, whatever they are, do not include the obtaining of appropriate M-facts. Now if we take any M-experience of this class to be the M-perception it seems to be, we shall *normally* be *mistaken* in our belief in the appropriate M-facts; for since its causes do not include the obtaining of appropriate M-facts, it could be no more than a flukish coincidence or outsize piece of luck if, nevertheless, appropriate M-facts did happen to obtain. Of any M-experience which belongs to this class, we may say that it is an essentially *undependable* M-experience.

If an M-experience belongs to this class, then it belongs to this class even if, as a matter of fact, appropriate M-facts do happen to obtain. And here, surely, is the rationale of the proposition that an M-experience is the M-perception it seems to be only if it is causally dependent on appropriate M-facts. The rationale lies in the conjunction of the two facts: (1) that if an M-experience occurs for which the dependence-condition does not hold, and if the subject of the experience believes in the appropriate M-facts, then he will normally be mistaken in that belief; and (2) that if he takes the M-experience to be the M-perception it seems to be, then he necessarily has that belief. So we would say in such a case that he is wrong in taking the M-experience to be the M-perception it seems to be even if, by a fluke, he happens to be right in his belief in the appropriate M-facts. The concept of perception is too closely linked to that of knowledge for us to tolerate the idea of someone's being in this way merely flukishly right in taking his M-experience to be the M-*perception* that it seems to be. Only those M-experiences which are in a certain sense dependable are to count as the M-perceptions they seem to be; and dependability in this sense entails dependence, causal or nonlogical dependence on appropriate M-facts.

It is obvious, however, that the foregoing only takes us, at best, a part of the way to understanding the place, in the notion of perception, of the notion of causal dependence of sensible experience on physical object perceived. For one thing I have so far been exclusively concerned with cases in which M-experience, M-perception (if any) and relevant M-facts (if any) are all specified in the same or corresponding terms. So the account falls sadly short of generality. For obviously I may perceive an X without its sensibly seeming to me just as if I am perceiving an X.

The way in which Grice stated his original conclusion, unlike the way I stated it, does not suffer from this lack of generality. What I said (and sought to explain) was: it is a necessary condition of an M-experience being the M-perception it seems to be that the experience should be causally dependent on appropriate M-facts. What he said was: It is a necessary condition of one's perceiving a material object that one's sense-impressions should be causally dependent on some state of affairs involving that object. Just because of its lack of generality my statement may seem to offer the promise, within its limits, of a very safe and simple step from necessary to necessary-and-sufficient conditions. Grice's statement, on the other hand, just because of its generality, cries out for supplementary *restrictions* to turn it into a statement of sufficient as well as necessary conditions. For obviously our sense-impressions may be causally dependent on states of affairs involving many material objects which we are not currently perceiving, such as our brains and eyes, electricity-generating plants and so on.

Grice's suggestion is that we should proceed by imposing appropriate restrictions on the *ways* or *modes* in which objects contribute causally to the occurrence of sense-impressions. We should not, he says, derive these restrictions from our specialised knowledge of the causal mechanisms of perception; for "if we are attempting to characterize the ordinary notion of perceiving, we should not explicitly introduce material of which someone who is perfectly capable of employing the ordinary notion may be ignorant."[2] Both this self-denying ordinance and the reason given for it are obviously sound in themselves. We may put the point, however, a little differently. The aim is to characterize the place of causation in a naive or nonspecialist concept of perception. Consequently we should not draw on any knowledge of the causal conditions of perception except such as may be implicit in the concept of perception in general or in the nonspecialist concepts of the different modes of perception.

Grice suggests that the kind of restriction required could be adequately indicated by the use of examples. Thus we might say that "for an object to be perceived by X it is sufficient that it should be causally involved in the generation of some sense-impression had by X in the kind of way in which, for example, when I look at my hand in a good light, my hand is causally responsible for its looking to me as if there were a hand before me, or in which . . . (and so on), *whatever that kind of way may be;* and to be enlightened on that question one must have recourse to the specialist."[3] To the example about the hand we are presumably to add other examples relating to other sensory modes of perception than the visual and, perhaps (though it is not quite clear whether this would be thought necessary), examples of artificially mediated perception as well. Clearly, however, we cannot be satisfied with this procedure unless we can at least state the general principles governing the selection of our examples. An unsympathetic critic might be inclined to say that it is impossible to

2. Op. cit., p. 143.
3. Op. cit., pp. 143–144.

state the general principle without revealing a circularity in the doctrine. For what qualifies the chosen example for a place in the list is nothing other than the fact that when someone is correctly described as looking at his hand in a good light, and having the impression, in part causally dependent on the presence of his hand, that he is seeing a hand before him, then he undoubtedly *is* seeing his hand. So the generalised statement of the doctrine comes to this: for an object to be perceived by X, it is sufficient that it should be causally involved in the generation of some sense-impression of X's in any one of the ways in which, *when X perceives an object,* that object is causally responsible for (or causally involved in the generation of) X's sense-impression. And this is unacceptably circular.

Perhaps this criticism is too unsympathetic. Reconsideration of Grice's chosen example suggests another way of exploiting the idea of imposing restrictions on modes of causal dependence. For his example is not simply an example of an undoubted M-perception. It is an example of a case in which M-experience, M-perception and M-facts are specified in the same terms. It is an example of an M-experience which is the M-perception it seems to be. Perhaps we can make use of this feature to obtain a characterization both general and noncircular of the required restriction.

We prepare for the attempt by returning to my own limited statement of the causal condition. That statement ran: it is a necessary condition of an M-experience being the M-perception it seems to be that the experience should be causally dependent on corresponding M-facts. We may be tempted for a moment to rewrite this straight away as a statement of necessary and sufficient conditions, i.e. to say: it is a necessary and sufficient condition of an M-experience being the M-perception it seems to be that the experience should be causally dependent on appropriate M-facts.

Before we yield to the temptation, however, we should reflect on the case of the capricious philosophical experimenter who, perhaps with a view to illustrating Grice's original point, deliberately contrives, by unusual means, to produce in his subject an M-experience which accords with the M-facts. Why should this make us pause? Isn't the point that the means he uses are such as would produce the M-experience even if the M-facts did not obtain? Yes; but notice that it is part of the description of the situation that the experimenter would not have produced that M-experience had those M-facts not obtained. So there is, after all, a kind of causal dependence of M-experience on M-facts. So the experimenter has not, after all, illustrated his point. But perhaps he has illustrated another point: viz. that causal dependence of M-experience on corresponding M-facts is not in general *sufficient* for M-perception.

Can we deal with the case by writing a negative provision into our limited statement of necessary and sufficient conditions? Well, we can try. We can rule the case out by declaring that causal dependence which runs through the will of a capricious intervener is not to count. Notice the qualification 'capricious'. It does not seem to be the fact that causal dependence runs through the will which makes it necessary (if it is necessary) to rule the case out; but rather the fact that the will is a capricious will. Suppose we imagine a noncapricious contriver, devoted and reliable, whose aim, perhaps, is to make up for the deficiencies of a percipient's perceptual experience, say his blindness. Let his technique be suggestion or cortical stimulation or what you will, only so long as he regularly produces no M-experiences but such as would normally occur in a percipient in his subject's environment. Do we have to imagine him replaced by a *machine*, as we might, in order to say that the percipient *sees* — with artificial aids? Is not one trusty medium as good as another, if it is equally trusty? In some philosophies, when dualism has got out of control, God is invoked as the trusty contriver of M-experiences in general; though, to be sure, this is a sign that dualism has got out of control.

Well, then, let us write a negative provision regarding the capricious will into our limited statement of necessary and sufficient conditions; and proceed. To do so, of course, is to leave a flank exposed; for if one such negative provision is necessary, might not others be necessary too? But we will worry about that later. For the moment we have a limited formula which, apart from the one negative provision, makes no reference to modes of causal dependence. But we have not achieved generality. Perhaps we can now achieve generality by introducing a reference to modes of causal dependence in the following way; (1) introduce the concept of the entire class of ways, or kinds of way, in which — the excluded case apart — M-experiences are causally dependent on appropriate (or corresponding) M-facts, when they are so dependent; and then (2) declare that it is a necessary and sufficient condition of any sensible experience being a perception of a material object that it is causally dependent on facts involving that material object in one of these ways or kinds of way.

I think there may well be more than one kind of objection to this suggestion. Remember our aim: it is to determine how the general notion of causal dependence of sensible experience on facts about material objects perceived fits into, or finds a place in, the naive concept of perception of material objects. The kind of objection I want briefly to develop turns on the thought that even the general and unspecific reference to *modes* of causal dependence contained in the two-part formula is, given this aim, unnecessary; and if it is unnecessary, it is obfuscating. What clearly is necessary is that we should somehow move towards generality, away from the limited case where M-experience and M-array or M-facts are specified in the same or corresponding terms. But what, we may ask, underlies the possibility of specifying them in *different* terms, as we can in so many cases of perception? What are the sources of possible difference or discrepancy, in cases of actual perception, between the specification of what it sensibly seems to one just as if one were perceiving and possible, correct specifications of what one *is* perceiving? There are, it seems, two general cases: I shall call them respectively the case of 'excess description' and the case of 'corrected description'.

The possibility of the first kind of case is obvious from the fact that M-experiences which are indeed the M-perceptions they seem to be are never *merely* the M-perceptions they seem to be. It sensibly seems to me as if I see a man; and I do see a man. He is a postman, perhaps, or a prime minister. So I see a postman (or a prime minister), even though my M-experience could not, we are to suppose, be truly characterized by saying that it sensibly seems to me just as if I see a postman (or a prime minister). It sensibly seems to me just as if I see a white object on the side of a hill. I do see such an object. It is a car. So I see a car on the side of the hill, even though my M-experience could not be characterized in these terms.

Is any reference to modes of causal dependence of sensible experience on states of affairs involving objects necessary to account for this kind of difference between sensible-experience-specification and perception-specification? Obviously none is. What makes the 'excess descriptions' correct statements of what is perceived is simply that they contain fuller identifications or further characterizations of the very objects or arrays referred to in that description of what one perceives which would follow from the fact that one's M-experience is *at least* the M-perception it seems to be.

What of the other general case, the case of the corrected description: the case in which the specification of the M-*experience* would include features or detail which would not figure in any correct specification of the M-*perception;* or, to put it differently, the case in which, if we believed our M-experience was at least the M-perception it seemed to be, we would be (at least in part) mistaken?

Let us think of any corrected description of what we perceive, considered in relation to the uncorrected description, as consisting of two constituents: a constituent which it has in common with the uncorrected description and a constituent which is incompatible with the uncorrected description. If it sensibly seems to me as if I perceive a blue cube before me (the uncorrected description) when I actually perceive a black cube before me (the corrected description), the common constituent of the corrected description is 'cube before me' and the incompatible constituent is the qualification 'black'. If we can take care of the common constituent, the incompatible constituent can be left to take care of itself; or, rather, can be regarded as already taken care of by the previous account of excess descriptions.

But we already have the means of taking care of the common constituent. We can see this as soon as we relate the case to our existing formula. Any relatively full or specific description of an M-experience entails or includes less full or more general descriptions of the same M-experience. If it is true that it sensibly seems to me just as if I perceive a blue cube before me, then it is also true that it sensibly seems to me just as if I see a cube before me. So we arrive at the following quite general statement or formula: any M-experience is *the most specific* M-perception it seems to be for which there obtain appropriate M-facts upon which the M-experience is causally or nonlogically dependent. The basic specification of material objects or arrays perceived follows from this specification of those M-facts. A fuller specification of those objects or arrays can be obtained in the way already indicated, by adding excess descriptions *au plaisir*. In all this there is no mention at all of kinds or modes of causal dependence of M-experience on states of affairs involving material objects perceived.

This formula seems to work reasonably well for cases of M-experiences which are in fact M-perceptions of some kind. Where an M-experience description requires *correction* to yield the corresponding M-perception description, the rule for correction works, as it were, automatically, with little risk of admitting inadmissible candidates for the role of object perceived. Still, little risk is not the same as no risk. Moreover, an obvious difficulty seems to arise in the case of M-experiences which are not M-perceptions at all, i.e. in the case of totally hallucinatory M-experiences. For any such experience is, doubtless, causally dependent on some state of the subject's brain. And of any such experience it is necessarily true that a description at the limit of nonspecificity can be given, viz. the description: it sensibly seems to the subject just as if he is perceiving some material object. So shall we not, in default of any other candidate for the role of object perceived, be forced by the formula to say that the subject is perceiving his own brain? As we shall see in a moment, the formula as it stands may allow, or seem to allow, for other candidates as well. But, by hypothesis, no candidates at all are admissible; for the M-experiences in question are not M-perceptions of any kind.

It might be hoped that this difficulty could be met by requiring some degree of sensible coincidence between an M-experience description and an M-array description as a condition of counting the M-experience described as a perception of the M-array described or of any object mentioned in describing that array. It might be said: M-experiences are perceptions only of those, among the material bodies upon which they nonlogically depend, of which they are sensibly representative; and while 'sensible representativeness' is certainly a matter of degree, the bare mention of 'some material body' in the description of an M-experience on the one hand, and of some objective state of affairs on the other, is insufficient to get us across the threshold of this concept.

The suggested requirement, however, at least on its most natural interpretation, is inadequate to its purpose. We need not pause to wonder where exactly the threshold of the concept of sensible representativeness lies. For if it is low enough to admit the cases we must admit, it is far too low to exclude the cases we must exclude. The hallucinated man, asked to describe his experience, *might* give just such a description as one would give who, in good observational conditions, was actually perceiving a human brain suspended before him by an invisible thread.

The difficulty regarding hallucinatory experience may take another form. Kinglake reports that, travelling in the deserts of the Near East, he 'heard' the church bells of his native English village. His experience was surely causally dependent upon past pealings of those bells.[4] Suppose, for simplicity's sake, that a single such pealing were responsible for such an experience, and let the condition of sensible representativeness be as richly satisfied as you please. The case must still be excluded. So, too, if Hamlet, or such a one, 'sees' — what is invisible to the rest of the world — a solid-looking apparition of his father, dressed as he formerly appeared on a single occasion of his now ended life. The experience may be causally dependent on the earlier fleshly appearance, but does not count as a perception of that appearance.

Must we, to avoid these difficulties, fall back on some form of that suggestion which I considered earlier and rejected? Must we, after all, incorporate in our formulae some general, nonspecifying reference to ways (to be revealed by natural science) in which objects are causally responsible for the generation of sense-impressions? One may reasonably jib at the suggestion. To bring in a wholly new type of consideration to deal with a tiny minority of peripheral cases is not only disappointingly inelegant, it is suspiciously so.

Let us return, then, to the formula lately arrived at and reconsider it in relation to the hallucinatory cases. The formula ran: any M-experience is the most specific M-perception it seems to be for which there obtain appropriate M-facts upon which the M-experience is causally or nonlogically dependent. The formula seems to work reasonably well for those

---

4. Kinglake's own diagnosis is worth quoting: "I attributed the effect to the great heat of the sun, the perfect dryness of the clear air through which I moved, and the deep stillness of all around me. It seemed to me that these causes, by occasioning a great tension, and consequent susceptibility of the hearing organs, had rendered them liable to tingle under the passing touch of some mere memory. . . ." (*Eothen*, ch. XVII).

M-experiences which are in fact M-perceptions, and then to break down completely and obviously for those that are not. Let us expand the sense of the formula a little. The idea is that any M-experience description contains an M-array description and entails a series of less specific M-experience descriptions containing less specific M-array descriptions. We work through this series until we come to the most specific M-array description which fits some actual M-array upon which the M-experience causally depends. We then declare the M-experience to the M-perception of the items mentioned in the description of that M-array.

The expansion suggests that what we need, to deal with our cases of hallucination, is some restriction on what is to count as a 'fit' between M-experience descriptions and M-facts. The restriction will scarcely be felt as such so long as we are dealing only with M-experiences which are indeed M-perceptions of some kind; but it must be mentioned explicitly to deal with those that are not. The mention of sensible representativeness was an attempt to introduce the required kind of restriction, but an unsuccessful attempt. Though some restriction of this kind may be necessary, it is not sufficient; for, as we saw, a hallucination, dependent on some state of the subject's brain, could be as *of* a brain, or a hallucination dependent upon a past pealing of bells could be as *of* a peal of bells of just such a musical quality.

Implicit in the naive concept of perception, however, are restrictions of a different kind. They relate, roughly speaking, to the temporal and spatial positioning, relative to the putative perceiver, of the items, events or situations mentioned in specifying the candidate M-facts. The naive concept of perception — unaided perception, that is — includes that of a perspective or 'view', from a certain *point* of view determined by the position and orientation of the appropriate organs of sense, on contemporary or near-contemporary states of the world. From this flow all sorts of tautologies, suitably diversified for different sense-modalities, in which the causal and the logical are inseparably intertwined, and in which there figure essentially the concepts of (1) *range* and (2) *masking* or *obstruction*. Thus, as regards range, we have the tautology that, however large the visible thing, if removed far enough away, it will be *out of sight;* and the smaller it is, the nearer is far enough. However loud the report of the cannon, if it is far enough away, it will be *out of earshot;* and the louder it is, the farther is far enough. One's own arc of vision is (contingently) limited, but (necessarily) one can only see what is within one's arc of vision. As regards masking or obstruction, we have the general truth that the perception of an object by a given sense, even though the object is not out of range of that sense, can be *obstructed* or the object *masked* by another object. One cannot see the skin through the clothes, unless they are see-through clothes; one can feel the muscles beneath the skin and even through the jerkin, but not through the plate-armour; the orders of the commander are audible through the sizzling of the fuse, but not through the explosion of the cannon. A suitable tautology could be drafted for every such case, and for every sense: e.g., given two sounds, each separately such as to be within earshot from a given place at a given time, then if one is loud-and-near enough and the other soft-and-distant enough, the first will drown the second.

It seems clear that it is in the light of such restrictions as these that the unhallucinated and unsophisticated observer decides, and has no difficulty in deciding, that there just are no fact-fitting candidates for membership in the appropriate series of M-array descriptions generated by the experience-report of the hallucinated subject. The hallucinated subject may describe an experience as of seeing a brain, and the experience is doubtless causally dependent on, *inter alia,* a contemporary state of his own brain; but he can't be seeing his brain, for his brain is not within his arc of vision and is masked by his cranium even from those within whose arc of vision it is. Hamlet, as his mother remarks, bends his corporeal eye on vacancy, hence on nothing, hence on no M-array at all. The past pealing of bells is disqualified by remoteness both in time and in space from supplying appropriate M-facts, though it supplies M-facts on which the experience causally depends.

Of course these requirements or restrictions are modified in various ways; but not in such ways as to displace them from the basic position they hold in the concept of sense-perception. Thus we recognize artificial means of reducing the limitations of unaided perception, of increasing, so to say, the range, refinement and penetration of our organs of perception. Or again, we allow perception of 'reproductions' to count as perception of originals: I *can* be said to perceive, indirectly, my own brain or the past pealing of remote bells; for I can perceive directly, *under* the mentioned restrictions, such things as X-ray photographs or recordings which are themselves sensibly representative of those originals and causally derivative from them in just this respect of sensible representativeness. But any notion of perception which is thus *aided* or *indirect* or both is clearly derivative from, or dependent on, the concept of direct or unaided perception.

Do these considerations solve the problem posed for our formula by the case of the totally hallucinatory experience? I think it might be said that while the relevance of these considerations is unchallengeable, the mode of presenting them is not. Challenge might come from two opposite directions. First, it might be said that there has been a surreptitious or unacknowledged reintroduction of the notion of the *ways* in which an M-experience may be causally dependent on states of affairs involving any material object of which it can be held to be a perception. The point of this criticism would be not that it was wrong to reintroduce that notion, but that it was wrong to disguise or conceal its reintroduction. Second, it might be said that I have represented the relevant restrictions regarding relation to the putative perceiver etc. as outside the scope of the concept of sensible representativeness; but they really fall within it.

Evidently, if either of these criticisms has weight, it weighs against the other. As regards the second, I shall say simply this: if anyone cares to reinterpret the notion of sensible representativeness in such a way as to include the relational restrictions in question, he has my consent. What of the first and countervailing criticism, which, from the point of view of the present argument, is the only one which constitutes an objection? *Has the notion of modes of causal dependence been reintroduced?*

In our ordinary references to the limitations I have mentioned, we say such things as these: that a certain thing is too far away for us to make it out, or that it is too small to be detected at this distance or that we are too short-sighted or that the intervening mist is too thick. Here, certainly, we speak of causal conditions of the possibility or impossibility of perception of such a thing. But it does not seem that there is any concealed, implicit reference, however unspecific, to modes or mechanisms of causal dependence such as natural science may ultimately make us acquainted with. *Perhaps* the point is a fine one, *perhaps* not ultimately settleable; for what, after all, is meant by 'a *way*' in which one thing is causally responsible for another? But, for my own part, I should be inclined to maintain a distinction between two things: (1) a specific concept, intrinsic to the naive concept of perception from-a-point-of-view, of the causal *conditions* under which a thing is accessible to perception, namely, that of being within unobstructed range of the relevant organ; and (2) the general idea of causal *ways or means* whereby a material object is causally responsible for producing the experience of perceiving it. It is clear that we have to refer to the former in discharging the task we set ourselves. It is not clear that we have to refer to the latter; and *if* we do, we refer to it only as a dependent of the previous concept and not as an independent factor.

However, the game is not over yet. Long ago I left a flank exposed. There was the case of the capricious will, the intervener who produced in his subject an M-experience which the informed judge would declare to be no M-perception at all, even though both the general condition of causal dependence was, in a way, satisfied and the conditions of accessibility which I have just been describing were satisfied as well. We noted that it was the capriciousness of the will which bothered the informed judge, who might be willing to speak of a form of artificially mediated perception so long as the arrangements, whatever they were, were dependable. But, capricious wills apart, might there not be other similar cases which the unsophisticated judge would take to be cases of perception but which the informed judge would declare was no such thing, would classify rather with Kinglake's hallucination? Surely this might be so if, owing to some complicated and fortuitous combination of physical circumstances, including perhaps some temporary quirk of neuro-physiological functioning, the causal route from M-fact to M-experience were sufficiently bizarre. I forbear to describe cases: the philosophical imagination will be ready enough to supply them. Their common point will be to demonstrate that reference to kinds of causal mechanism is, after all, necessary; for what will rule out the imagined cases from counting as cases of perception is the fact that the causal route is the wrong kind of route, that the causal dependence is not in an acceptable mode.

But we must distinguish. We must distinguish between the naive or unsophisticated concept of perception and the modifications and refinements that the concept undergoes as knowledge increases and technology advances. The acquisition and progressive increase of knowledge of the normal natural mechanisms of perception, and of the technical possibilities of supplementing them, may well lead us to set up standards in the light of which we would disqualify some imaginable causal routes as too freakish or irregular, or too little amenable to control or exploitation, to qualify as perceptual routes. I do not deny that the enriched or modified concept which permits us to imagine such routes and to make such discriminations is superior to the naive concept which is blank on the subject. I only say that they are different, that one concept is a development from the other. The development is natural enough, of course, as soon as we ask the question 'How?' And that question is natural enough once an inquiring mind applies itself to our primitive concept of the causal conditions of perception. My point is that there is room for an adequate working concept of perception and its modes in heads which that question has never even entered; and the existence of such a concept is a precondition of that question entering any head at all.

It might now be said: if the concept of perception we are concerned with has this degree of innocence, is it even right to find implicit in it the general idea that causal dependence of M-experience on facts involving the object perceived is a necessary condition of the experience counting as a perception of the object? I think so: for various reasons. Here is one, which should suffice. It would require little enough calculation for that rugged soldier, Macbeth, who rightly identified his M-experience as a false creation proceeding from the heat-oppressed brain, to appreciate that the additional fact of an actual dagger there which made no difference, would make no difference; or for his wife's nurse to appreciate that she couldn't cure Lady Macbeth's delusion ('Here's the smell of the blood still') simply by spreading some actual blood on her hands.

The position I have defended receives, perhaps, some reinforcement from consideration of another, quite different, minor difficulty. There are cases, it might be said, in which the subject undoubtedly is perceiving a material object, but his sensible experience is not properly described as an *M*-experience at all. Thus it might be the case that a subject's sensible experience was most aptly described by saying that it sensibly seemed to him just as if he was perceiving a deep black shadow when he was in fact perceiving a piece of black cloth which looked like a shadow. The case is perhaps a little dubious, but let us admit it. Then let us point out that a shadow, though not a material object, is a public phenomenal object, and so belongs, together with perceptible material objects, to the wider class of public perceptual objects. Then cases of this kind, together with their perhaps more frequent converses (in which it sensibly seems to one who is in fact perceiving a phenomenal object as if he were perceiving a material object) can readily be accommodated in a widened formula in which the notion of a material object is replaced by that of public perceptual object, comprehending the material and the merely phenomenal alike. Thus throughout our formulae we may replace 'M-experience', 'M-array', 'M-perception' etc. by 'P-experience', 'P-array', 'P-perception' etc., where 'P' stands for 'public perceptual object' just as 'M' stands for 'material object'. Apart from cases in which the material appears as phenomenal or the phenomenal as material, there is a clear gain in generality here, particularly as regards the sense of hearing; for we often find it more natural to speak of hearing, say, a whistle or a roar rather than of hearing something or somebody whistling or roaring. Indeed I partially anticipated this extension in speaking earlier of the conditions of audibility of sounds.

Our wider formula, like our narrower formula, requires the existence of the object perceived, phenomenal or material, to be a nonlogically necessary condition of any experience which can correctly be described as a perception of it. The lately mentioned restrictions regarding range and masking apply, *mutatis mutandis,* to phenomenal as to material candidates for the role of object perceived. For sounds can be drowned by other sounds, shadows masked by the objects which cast them, etc. But there is minimal temptation, in the case of phenomenal objects, to regard mention of these restrictions as containing a covert reference to ways or means whereby such an object is causally responsible for producing the experience of perceiving it. It will be said that this is simply because it makes no sense to raise the question by what means sounds, for example, produce the experience of hearing them; for sounds are nothing but *audibilia;* and, in general, this form of question has no application to merely phenomenal, as opposed to material, objects. We may grant the point; but should note that it leaves untouched, if it does not emphasize, another point: the perfectly general point that reference to conditions, relating to range and masking, under which a perceptible object in general is accessible to perception from a certain position need not of itself import a covert reference to means, known or unknown, by which the object produces the experience of perceiving it.

Charles A. Baylis:
A Bibliography

C. L. Reid, *compiler*
Youngstown State University

"Internality and Interdependence." *Journal of Philosophy*, 26, no. 14 (July 4, 1929), 373–379.

"The Philosophical Functions of Emergence." *Philosophical Review*, 38, no. 4 (July, 1929), 372–384.

"Meanings and their Exemplification." *Journal of Philosophy*, 27, no. 7 (March 27, 1930), 169–174.

"Implication and Subsumption." *Monist*, 41, no. 3 (July, 1931), 392–399.

"A Calculus of Propositional Concepts" (with Albert A. Bennett). *Mind*, 44, no. 174 (April, 1935), 152–167.

"The Nature of Evidential Weight." *Journal of Philosophy*, 32, no. 11 (May 23, 1935), 281–286.

"Are Some Propositions Neither True nor False?" *Philosophy of Science*, 3, no. 2 (April, 1936), 156–166.

Formal Logic (with Albert A. Bennett). New York: Prentice-Hall, 1939.

"How to Make Our Ideas Clearer." *Journal of Philosophy*, 37, no. 9 (April 25, 1940), 225–232.

Review of Warner Arms Wick: *Metaphysics and the New Logic*. *Philosophy and Phenomenological Research*, 4, no. 1 (Sept., 1943), 106–108.

"Critical Comments on the Symposium on Meaning and Truth." *Philosophy and Phenomenological Research*, 5, no. 1 (Sept., 1944), 80–93.

Descriptive notice of Z. Jordan: *The Development of Mathematical Logic and Logical Positivism in Poland Between the Two Wars*. *Philosophical Review*, 55, no. 4 (July, 1946), 494.

Review of Hubert G. Alexander: *Time as Dimension and History*. *Philosophical Review*, 56, no. 1 (Jan., 1947), 113–114.

Review of C. I. Lewis: *An Analysis of Knowledge and Valuation*. *Philosophy and Phenomenological Research*, 8, no. 1 (Sept., 1947), 152–159.

"Critical Comments on Professor Fitch's Article 'On God and Immortality.'" *Philosophy and Phenomenological Research*, 8, no. 4 (June, 1948), 694–697.

"Facts, Propositions, Exemplification and Truth." *Mind,* 57, no. 228 (Oct., 1948), 459–479.

"The Given and Perceptual Knowledge," in *Philosophic Thought in France and the United States,* ed. Marvin Farber. U. of Buffalo Publications in Philosophy, Buffalo, 1950, pp. 443–461.

"Rational Preference, Determinism and Moral Obligation." *Journal of Philosophy,* 47, no. 3 (Feb. 2, 1950), 57–63.

Review of F. C. Sharp: *Good Will and Ill Will. Journal of Philosophy,* 48, no. 9 (April 26, 1951), 301–306.

"Universals, Communicable Knowledge and Metaphysics." *Journal of Philosophy,* 48, no. 21 (Oct. 11, 1951), 636–644.

"The Confirmation of Value Judgments." *Philosophical Review,* 61, no. 1 (Jan., 1952), 50–58.

"Comments on Symposium on Utilitarianism and Moral Obligation." *Philosophical Review,* 61, no. 3 (July, 1952), 327–330.

"Intrinsic Goodness." *Philosophy and Phenomenological Research,* 13, no. 1 (Sept., 1952), 15–27.

Review of David Baumgardt: *Bentham and the Ethics of Today. Philosophical Review,* 63, no. 1 (Jan., 1954), 102–106.

Review of C. D. Broad: *Ethics and the History of Philosophy: Selected Essays. Philosophical Review,* 63, no. 3 (July, 1954), 431–432.

Review of A. J. Ayer: *Philosophical Essays. Philosophical Review,* 64, no. 4 (Oct., 1955), 640–644.

Review of Philip Blair Rice: *On the Knowledge of Good and Evil. Philosophical Review,* 66, no. 2 (April, 1957), 261–268.

"Logical Subjects and Physical Objects." *Philosophy and Phenomenological Research,* 17, no. 4 (June, 1957), 483–487.

Ethics: Principles of Wise Choice. New York: Holt, Rinehart and Winston, 1958.

"Grading, Values and Choice." *Mind,* 67, no. 268 (Oct., 1958), 485–501.

"Professor Chisholm on Perceiving." *Journal of Philosophy,* 56, no. 20 (Sept. 24, 1959), 773–791.

"Normative Ethics and Empirical Knowledge," in *Horizons of a Philosopher: Essays in Honor of David Baumgardt,* ed. Joseph Frank, Helmut Minkowski and Ernest J. Steinglass. Leiden: E. J. Brill, 1963, pp. 16–33.

"C. I. Lewis's Theory of Value and Ethics." *Journal of Philosophy,* 61, no. 19 (Oct. 15, 1964), 559–567.

Metaphysics (editor). New York: Macmillan, 1965.

"Immorality, Crime and Treatment," in *Philosophical Perspectives on Punishment,* ed. E. H. Madden, R. Handy and M. Farber, from lectures given at SUNY, Buffalo on October 7, 1966. American Lecture

Series #697, Bannerstone Division of American Lectures in Philosophy. Springfield, Ill.: Charles C. Thomas, 1966.

"Perception and Sensations as Presentational," in *Current Philosophical Issues* (Ducasse Festschrift), ed. Frederick C. Dommeyer. American Lecture Series #657, Springfield, Ill.: Charles C. Thomas, 1966.

"Perception." *Southern Journal of Philosophy,* 4, no. 3 (Fall, 1966), 117–122.

Review of Arthur E. Murphy: *The Theory of Practical Reason. Philosophical Review,* 76, no. 4 (Oct., 1967), 511–515.

"Lewis's Theory of Facts," in *The Philosophy of C. I. Lewis,* ed. Paul A. Schilpp. LaSalle, Ill.: Open Court Publishing Co., 1968.

Review of Roderick Chisholm: *Theory of Knowledge. Philosophy and Phenomenological Research,* 28, no. 4 (June, 1968), 600–601.

Contributors

Robert Binkley is chairman of the department of Philosophy at the University of Western Ontario. He has taught at Duke University, and has been a Fulbright Fellow at Oxford. He is co-editor of *Agent, Action, and Reason;* his philosophic interests center about the philosophy of mind, philosophy of logic, and moral philosophy.

Hector-Neri Castañeda has taught at Duke University, at Wayne State University, and has been visiting professor of philosophy at the University of Texas at Austin and at the University of Western Ontario. He is presently professor of Philosophy at Indiana University. He is the founding editor of *Nous*. He has worked widely and intensively in metaphysics, epistemology, philosophy of mind, and moral philosophy. Besides numerous philosophical essays he has published *The Structure of Morality, La Dialectica de la Conciencia de se Mismo,* and he has edited and contributed to *Morality and the Language of Conduct*. In 1967 he held a Guggenheim Fellowship.

Romane L. Clark is professor of Philosophy and chairman of the department of Philosophy at Indiana University. He has taught also at Duke University and at the University of Western Ontario. His philosophical interests are in philosophy of mind, philosophy of logic and theory of knowledge. He is co-editor of *Introduction to Logic*.

John Heintz has taught at the University of North Carolina at Chapel Hill and is presently chairman and professor of Philosophy at the University of Calgary. He is the author of *Subject and Predicables*. His philosophical interests are in metaphysics, logic, and philosophy of logic.

John Lachs was born in Budapest, Hungary, and has taught at the College of William and Mary and since 1967 at Vanderbilt University where he is professor of Philosophy. His numerous published articles deal principally with topics in metaphysics and perception. He is the author of *Animal Faith and Spiritual Life: Unpublished and Uncollected Works of George Santyana,* and *Marxist Philosophy: A Bibliographical Guide*. He was awarded a research grant in 1972–73 by the National Endowment for the Humanities.

Robert L. Patterson, now emeritus professor of Philosophy at Duke University, has taught also at The Johns Hopkins University. He is the author of *The Conception of God in the Philosophy of Aquinas, The Philosophy of William Ellery Channing,* and *Irrationalism and Rationalism in Religion.* His essay in this volume reflects his further thoughts on the last of these topics.

Evan Simpson is associate professor of Philosophy at McMaster University where he has taught since 1966. His published articles have dealt mostly with skepticism, human action, and social facts. He is now completing a book, *Appraisal,* for which the article in this volume is an early study.

P. F. Stawson, former Fellow of University College, Oxford, is Waynflete Professor of Metaphysical Philosophy in the University of Oxford, and Fellow of Magdalen College. He is the author of *Introduction to Logical Theory, Individuals,* and *The Bounds of Sense.* He has taught in this country as visiting professor of Philosophy at Duke University and at Princeton University.

Erik Stenius was born in Helsinki, Finland. He has been lecturer in Philosophy and full professor at Abo Academy, and since 1963 has been professor of Philosophy at the University of Helsinki. He has taught as visiting professor at Duke University and at the State University of Iowa. His best known philosophical works are *Tankens Gryning (The Dawn of Thought),* a book on the pre-Socratics; *Wittgenstein's Tractatus: A Critical Exposition;* and *Critical Essays.* His philosophical interests have centered about the philosophy of language, but he has considerable interest in the history of philosophy, the philosophy of logic, and foundational questions in moral philosophy.

Paul Welsh is professor of Philosophy and chairman of the department of Philosophy at Duke University. He has also taught at Cornell University and at the State University of Iowa. His principle philosophic interests are in the philosophy of language, aesthetics, and moral philosophy. He is the co-editor of *Introduction to Logic.*

N. L. Wilson was born in Vancouver, British Columbia, has taught at Bishop's University and the University of Western Ontario, at Duke and at Harvard University (as visitor), and currently at McMasters University where he is professor of Philosophy. He has published a book, *The Concept of Language,* and a number of articles, most of which, like the contribution to the present volume, are concerned with the nature of reality as revealed through our language.